EA

FRIENDS
OF ACPL

796.3   R67

Rookie coaches baseball
guide

P9-BZL-565

# ROOKIE COACHES
# BASEBALL
## GUIDE

## American Coaching Effectiveness Program

officially endorsed by
**USA Baseball**

**Human Kinetics Publishers**
Champaign, Illinois

## Library of Congress Cataloging-in-Publication Data

Rookie coaches baseball guide : American Coaching Effectiveness
  Program, officially endorsed by USA Baseball.
    p.  cm.
   ISBN 0-87322-414-0
   1.  Baseball for children--Coaching.
  GV880.4.R66  1993
  796.357'083--dc20                        92-29519
                                             CIP

ISBN: 0-87322-414-0

Copyright © 1993 by Human Kinetics Publishers, Inc.

All rights reserved. Except for use in a review, the reproduction or utilization of this work in any form or by any electronic, mechanical, or other means, now known or hereafter invented, including xerography, photocopying, and recording, and in any information storage and retrieval system, is forbidden without the written permission of the publisher.

Figure 6.6 and 6.7 are from *Coaching Baseball Effectively* (pp. 9 and 32, respectively) by Steven D. Houseworth. Copyright 1986 by Human Kinetics Publishers, Inc. Reprinted by permission. Figures 7.3 and 8.4 are from *Coaching Pitchers* (pp. 63, 100) by Joe McFarland. Copyright 1990, 1985 by Joe McFarland. Reprinted by permission. Figure 7.6 is from *Coaching Baseball* (p. 153) by Bragg A. Stockton. Copyright 1984, 1979 by Bragg A. Stockton. Reprinted by permission. Figure 7.19 is from *Hit and Run Baseball* (p. 24) by Rod Delmonico. Copyright 1992 by Rod Delmonico. Reprinted by permission. Figure 7.22 is from *Rookie Coaches Softball Guide* (p. 54) by the American Coaching Effectiveness Program. Copyright 1992 by Human Kinetics Publishers, Inc. Reprinted by permission.

Developmental Editor: Ted Miller; Managing Editor: Jan Colarusso Seeley; Baseball Consultant: Dick Naylor, Hanover College; Assistant Editors: Laura Bofinger, Lisa Sotirelis; Copyeditor: Karen Dorman; Proofreader: Stefani Day; Production Director: Ernie Noa; Typesetter: Julie Overholt; Text Design: Keith Blomberg; Text Layout: Tara Welsch; Cover Design: Jack Davis; Cover Photo: John Kilroy/Photo Concepts; Illustrations: Tim Offenstein, Tim Stiles, Gretchen Walters; Printer: United Graphics

Human Kinetics books are available at special discounts for bulk purchase for sales promotions, premiums, fund-raising, or educational use. Special editions or book excerpts can also be created to specification. For details, contact the Special Sales Manager at Human Kinetics.

Printed in the United States of America    10  9  8  7  6  5  4  3  2

**Human Kinetics Publishers**
Box 5076, Champaign, IL 61825-5076
1-800-747-4457

*Canada:* Human Kinetics Publishers, P.O. Box 2503, Windsor, ON N8Y 4S2
1-800-465-7301 (in Canada only)

*Europe:* Human Kinetics Publishers (Europe) Ltd., P.O. Box IW14,
Leeds LS16 6TR, England
0532-781708

*Australia:* Human Kinetics Publishers, P.O. Box 80, Kingswood 5062,
South Australia
618-374-0433

*New Zealand:* Human Kinetics Publishers, P.O. Box 105-231,
Auckland 1
(09) 309-2259

Allen County Public Library
900 Webster Street
PO Box 2270
Fort Wayne, IN 46801-2270

# Contents

# A Message From USA Baseball

s the Executive Director and CEO of USA Baseball, I applaud your commitment to helping young Americans learn the fun and rewarding game of baseball. As a coach, you will have the opportunity to introduce youngsters to a sport that they will enjoy all of their lives, as well as one they will pass on to future generations of players and fans.

The *Rookie Coaches Baseball Guide* will be an invaluable resource for you. The practical, step-by-step information provided will prepare you for the task at hand of communicating the fundamentals of baseball to today's youth. You'll understand the importance of your role as a coach; how to communicate effectively with your players; the best way to teach new skills and organize on-field drills; how to promote team spirit and leadership; and basic first aid and sport science concepts.

The *Rookie Coaches Baseball Guide* gives you the fundamentals of the great game of baseball. By following the information provided in this guide, and keeping the FUN in FUNdamentals, you will provide young players with the ideals of teamwork, fitness, and friendship.

On behalf of USA Baseball and all of amateur baseball, I welcome you to coaching and wish you fun and the personal gratification that comes from working closely with our nation's future.

**Richard W. Case**
Executive Director and CEO
USA Baseball

# *Welcome to Coaching!*

**C**oaching young people is an exciting way to be involved in sport. But it isn't easy. Some coaches are overwhelmed by the responsibilities involved in helping athletes through their early sport experiences. And that's not surprising, because coaching youngsters requires more than bringing the bats and balls to the field and letting them play. It involves preparing them physically and mentally to compete effectively, fairly, and safely in their sport, and providing them a positive role model.

This book will help you meet the challenges *and* experience the many rewards of coaching young athletes. We call it the *Rookie Coaches Baseball Guide* because it is intended for adults with little or no formal preparation in coaching baseball. In this *Rookie Guide* you'll learn how to apply general coaching principles and teach baseball rules, skills, and strategies successfully to kids. And while you may find that some of the information does not apply to your amateur baseball program, we're confident this guide will help you get a good jump on your coaching career.

The American Coaching Effectiveness Program (ACEP) thanks USA Baseball and Coach Dick Naylor of Hanover College for contributing their baseball expertise to this book. Combined with ACEP's material on important coaching principles, this *Rookie Coaches Guide* covers all the bases.

This book also serves as a text for ACEP's Rookie Coaches Course. If you would like more information about this course or ACEP, please contact us at

ACEP
Box 5076
Champaign, IL 61825-5076
1-800-747-5698

Good Coaching!

# UNIT 1

# *Who, Me . . . a Coach?*

If you're like most youth league coaches, you were recruited from the ranks of concerned parents, sport enthusiasts, or community volunteers. And, like many rookie *and* veteran coaches, you probably have had little formal instruction on how to coach. But when the call went out for coaches to assist with the local youth baseball program, you answered because you like children, enjoy baseball, are community-minded, and perhaps are interested in starting a coaching career.

## *I Want to Help, But...*

Your initial coaching assignment may be difficult. Like many volunteers, you may not know everything there is to know about baseball, or about how to work with children between the ages of 6 and 14. Relax; this *Rookie Coaches Baseball Guide* will help you learn the basics for coaching baseball effectively. In the coming pages you will find the answers to such common questions as these:

- What tools do I need to be a good coach?

1

- How can I best communicate with my players?
- How do I go about teaching sport skills?
- What can I do to promote safety?
- What do I do when someone is injured?
- What are the basic rules, skills, and strategies of baseball?
- What practice drills will improve my players' baseball skills?

Before answering these questions, let's take a look at what's involved in being a coach.

## Am I a Parent or a Coach?

Many coaches are parents, but the two roles should not be confused. As a parent you are responsible only to yourself and your child; as a coach you are responsible to the organization, all the players on the team (including your child), and their parents.

Because of these additional responsibilities, your behavior on the baseball diamond will be different than it is at home, and your son or daughter may not understand why. Take these steps to avoid problems when coaching your child:

- Ask your child if she or he wants you to coach the team.
- Explain why you want to be involved with the team.
- Discuss with your child your new responsibilities and how they will affect your relationship when coaching.
- Limit your "coach" behavior to those times when you are in a coaching role.
- Avoid parenting during practice or game situations to keep your role clear in your child's mind.
- Reaffirm your love for your child irrespective of his or her performance on the baseball diamond.

## What Are My Responsibilities as a Coach?

A coach assumes the responsibility of doing everything possible to ensure that the youngsters on her or his team will have an enjoyable and safe sporting experience while they learn sport skills. If you're ever in doubt about your approach, remind yourself that "fun and fundamentals" are most important.

### Provide an Enjoyable Experience

Baseball should be fun. Even if nothing else is accomplished, make certain your players have fun. Take the fun out of baseball and you'll take the kids out of the sport.

Children enter sport for a number of reasons (e.g., to meet and play with other children, to develop physically, to learn skills), but their major objective is to have fun. Help them satisfy this goal by injecting humor and variety into your practices. Also, make games nonthreatening, festive experiences for your players. Such an approach will increase their desire to participate in the future, which should be the primary goal of youth sport.

Unit 2 teaches you how to satisfy your players' yearning for fun and keep winning in perspective. Unit 3 describes how to communicate this perspective effectively to your players.

## Provide a Safe Experience

You are responsible for planning and teaching activities in such a way that the progression between activities minimizes risks (see Units 4 and 5). You also must ensure that the facility where your team practices and plays and the equipment they use are free of hazards. Finally, you need to protect yourself from any issues of legal liability that might arise from your involvement as a coach. Unit 5 helps you take the appropriate precautions.

## Teach Basic Baseball Skills

In becoming a coach, you take on the role of educator. You must teach your players the fundamental skills and strategies necessary for success in baseball. That means that you need to "go to school." If you don't know the basics of baseball now, you can learn them by reading the second half of this guide. And even if you know baseball as a player, do you know how to teach it? This book helps you get started.

You'll also find that you are better able to teach the baseball skills and strategies you do know if you plan your practices. Unit 4 provides some guidelines for planning effective practices.

And many valuable baseball books are available, including those offered by Human Kinetics Publishers. See the list of books in the back of this guide or call 1-800-747-4457 for more information.

## Where Do I Get Help?

Veteran coaches in your league are an especially good source of information and assistance. These coaches have experienced the same emotions and concerns you are facing; their advice and feedback can be invaluable as you work through your first few seasons of coaching.

You can also learn a lot by observing local high school and college baseball coaches in practices and games. You might even ask a few of the coaches you respect most to lend a hand with a couple of your practices.

You can get additional help by attending baseball clinics, reading baseball publications, and studying instructional videos. Contact the American Coaching Effectiveness Program and the following national baseball organizations for more coaching information.

American Amateur Baseball Congress
P.O. Box 467
Marshall, MI 49068
(616) 781-2002

American Baseball Coaches Association
P.O. Box 665
North Amherst, MA 01059
(413) 549-2626

American Legion Baseball
P.O. Box 1055
Indianapolis, IN 46204
(317) 635-8411

Dixie Baseball, Inc.
P.O. Box 222
Lookout Mountain, TN 37350
(615) 821-6811

Little League Baseball, Inc.
P.O. Box 3485
Williamsport, PA 17701
(717) 326-1921

National Amateur Baseball Federation
12406 Keynote Ln.
Bowie, MD 20715
(301) 495-6950

National Police Athletic League
200 Castlewood Dr.
North Palm Beach, FL 33408
(407) 844-1823

PONY Baseball
P.O. Box 225
Washington, PA 15301
(412) 225-1060

USA Baseball
2160 Greenwood Ave.
Trenton, NJ 08609
(609) 586-2381

Coaching baseball is a rewarding experience. And, just as you want your players to learn and practice to be the best they can be, you need to learn all you can about coaching in order to be the best baseball coach you can be.

# UNIT 2

# *What Tools Do I Need to Coach?*

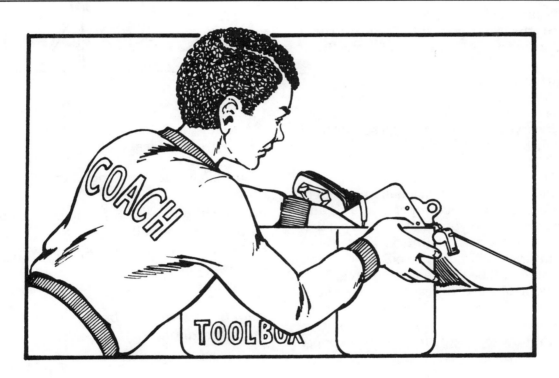

ave you acquired the traditional coaching tools— things like bats, balls, coaching shoes, a clipboard, and a scorebook? They'll help you coach, but to be a successful coach you'll need five other *tools* that cannot be bought. These tools are available only through self-examination and hard work, but they're easy to remember with the acronym COACH:

**C**—Comprehension

**O**—Outlook

**A**—Affection

**C**—Character

**H**—Humor

## *Comprehension*

*Comprehension* of the rules, skills, and tactics of baseball is required. To help you learn about the game, the second half of this guide describes how baseball is played as well as specific techniques and strategies. In the baseball-specific section of this guide, you'll also find a variety of drills to use in developing young players' skills. And, perhaps most important, you'll learn how to apply your knowledge of the game to teach your baseball team.

To improve your comprehension of baseball, take the following steps:

- Read the sport-specific section of this book.
- Read other baseball coaching books, including those available from ACEP (see the last page of this *Guide* to order).
- Contact any of the organizations listed on page 4.
- Attend baseball coaches' clinics.
- Talk with other, more experienced baseball coaches.
- Observe local college, high school, and youth baseball games.
- Watch televised baseball games.

In addition to having baseball knowledge, you must implement proper training and safety methods so your players can participate with little risk of injury. Even then, sport injuries will occur. And, more often than not, you'll be the first person responding to your players' injuries. So make sure you understand the basic emergency care procedures described in Unit 5. Also read in that unit how to handle more serious sport injury situations.

## Outlook

This coaching tool refers to your perspective and goals—what you are seeking as a coach. The most common coaching objectives are (a) to have fun, (b) to help players develop their physical, mental, and social skills, and (c) to win. Thus *outlook* involves your priorities, your planning, and your vision for the future.

To work successfully with children in a sport setting, you must have your priorities in order. In what order do you rank the importance of fun, development, and winning?

Answer the following questions to examine your objectives.

*Of which situation would you be most proud?*
a. Knowing that each participant enjoyed playing baseball
b. Seeing that all players improved their baseball skills
c. Winning the league championship

*Which statement best reflects your thoughts about sport?*
a. If it isn't fun, don't do it.
b. Everyone should learn something every day.
c. Sport isn't fun if you don't win.

*How would you like your players to remember you?*
a. As a coach who was fun to play for
b. As a coach who developed good fundamental skills in players
c. As a coach who had a winning record

*Which would you most like to hear said by a parent of a child on your team?*
a. Billy really had a good time playing baseball this year.

b. Maria learned some important lessons playing baseball this year.

c. Jake played on the first-place baseball team this year.

*Which of the following would be the most rewarding moment of your season?*

a. Having your team not want to stop playing even after practice is over

b. Seeing your players finally master the skill of striding forward and not bailing out in the batter's box

c. Winning the league championship

Look over your answers. If you most often selected ''a'' responses, then having fun is more important to you. A majority of ''b'' answers suggests that skill development is what attracts you to coaching. And if ''c'' was your most frequent response, winning tops your list of coaching priorities.

Most coaches say fun and development are more important, but when actually coaching, some coaches emphasize—indeed overemphasize— winning. You will also face situations that challenge you to keep winning in its proper perspective. During such moments you'll have to choose between emphasizing your players' development and winning. If your priorities are in order, your players' well-being will take precedence over your team's win-loss record every time.

Take the following actions to better define your outlook:

1. Determine your priorities for the season.
2. Prepare for situations that challenge your priorities.
3. Set goals for yourself and your players that are consistent with those priorities.
4. Plan how you and your players can best attain those goals.
5. Review your goals frequently to be sure that you are staying on track.

It is particularly important for coaches to permit all young athletes to participate. Each youngster should have an opportunity to develop skills and have fun—even if it means sacrificing a win or two during the season. After all, wouldn't you prefer losing a couple of games to losing a couple of players' interest in baseball?

Remember that the challenge and joy of sport is experienced through *striving to win*, not through winning itself. Players who aren't allowed off the bench are denied the opportunity to strive to win. And herein lies the irony: A coach who allows all of his or her players to participate and develop skills will—in the end—come out on top.

ACEP has a motto that will help you keep your outlook in the best interest of the kids on your team. It summarizes in four words all you need to remember when establishing your coaching priorities:

*Athletes First, Winning Second*

This motto recognizes that striving to win is an important, even vital, part of sport. But it emphatically states that no efforts in striving to win should be made at the expense of athletes' well-being, development, and enjoyment.

## Affection

This is another vital tool you will want to have in your coaching kit: a genuine concern for the young people you coach. *Affection* involves having a love for children, a desire to share with them your love and knowledge of sport, and the patience and understanding that allows all children playing for you to grow from their involvement in baseball.

Successful coaches have a real concern for the health and welfare of their players. They care that each child on the team has an enjoyable and successful experience. They have a strong desire to work with children and be involved in their growth. And they have the patience to work with those who are slower to learn or less capable of performing. If you have such qualities or are willing to work hard to develop them, then you have the *affection* necessary to coach young athletes.

There are many ways to demonstrate your affection and patience:

• Make an effort to get to know each player on your team.

- Treat each player as an individual.
- Empathize with players trying to learn new and difficult baseball skills.
- Treat players as you would like to be treated under similar circumstances.
- Be in control of your emotions.
- Show your enthusiasm for being involved with your team.
- Keep an upbeat and positive tone in all of your communications.

## Character

Youngsters learn by listening to what adults say. But they learn even more by watching the behaviors of certain important individuals. As a coach, you are likely to be a significant figure in the lives of your players. Will you be a good role model?

Having good *character* means modeling appropriate behaviors for sport and life. That means more than just saying the right things. What you say and what you do must match. There is no place in coaching for the "Do as I say, not as I do" philosophy. Be in control of yourself before, during, and after

all games and practices. And don't be afraid to admit that you were wrong. No one is perfect!

Consider the following steps to being a good role model:

- Take stock of your strengths and weaknesses.
- Build on your strengths.
- Set goals for yourself to improve upon those areas you would not like to see mimicked.
- Apologize to your team and to yourself if you slip up. You'll do better next time.

## Humor

*Humor* is often overlooked as a coaching tool. For our use it means having the ability to laugh *at* yourself and *with* your players during practices and games. Nothing helps balance the tone of a serious, skill-learning session like a chuckle or two. And a sense of humor puts in perspective the many mistakes your young players will make. So don't get upset over each miscue or respond negatively to erring players. Allow your players and yourself to enjoy the "ups," and don't dwell on the "downs."

Here are some tips for injecting humor into your practices:

- Make practices fun by including a variety of activities.
- Keep all players involved in drills and scrimmages.
- Consider laughter by your players a sign of enjoyment, not a lack of discipline.
- Smile!

## Where Do You Stand?

To take stock of your "coaching tool kit," rank yourself on each of these questions concerning the five coaching tools. Simply circle the number that best describes your *present* status on each item.

| Not at all | | Somewhat | | Very much so |
|---|---|---|---|---|
| 1 | 2 | 3 | 4 | 5 |

### Comprehension

1. Could you explain the rules of baseball to other parents without studying for a long time?            1 2 3 4 5
2. Do you know how to organize and conduct safe baseball practices?            1 2 3 4 5
3. Do you know how to provide first aid for most common, minor sport injuries?            1 2 3 4 5

*Comprehension Score:* _____

### Outlook

4. Do you keep winning in its proper perspective when you coach?            1 2 3 4 5
5. Do you plan for every meeting, practice, and game?            1 2 3 4 5
6. Do you have a vision of what you want your players to be able to do by the end of the season?            1 2 3 4 5

*Outlook Score:* _____

### Affection

7. Do you enjoy working with children?            1 2 3 4 5
8. Are you patient with youngsters learning new skills?            1 2 3 4 5
9. Are you able to show your players that you care?            1 2 3 4 5

*Affection Score:* _____

### Character

10. Are your words and behaviors consistent with each other?            1 2 3 4 5
11. Are you a good model for your players?            1 2 3 4 5
12. Do you keep negative emotions under control before, during, and after games?            1 2 3 4 5

*Character Score:* _____

### Humor

13. Do you usually smile at your players?            1 2 3 4 5
14. Are your practices fun?            1 2 3 4 5
15. Are you able to laugh at your mistakes?            1 2 3 4 5

*Humor Score:* _____

If you scored 9 or less on any of the coaching tools, be sure to reread those sections carefully. And even if you scored 15 on each tool, don't be complacent. Keep learning! Then you'll be well-equipped with the tools you need to coach young athletes.

# UNIT 3

# *How Should I Communicate With My Players?*

EVERYBODY GOT THAT?

ow you know the tools needed to COACH: Comprehension, Outlook, Affection, Character, and Humor. These are essential for effective coaching, and without them you'd have a difficult time getting started. But none of these tools will work if you don't know how to use them with your athletes—that requires skillful communication. This unit examines what communication is and how you can become a more effective communicator-coach.

## What's Involved in Communication?

Coaches often believe that communication involves only instructing players to do something, but these verbal commands are a very small part of the communication process.

More than half of what is communicated in a message is nonverbal. So when you are coaching, remember that "actions speak louder than words."

Communication in its simplest form involves two people: a *sender* and a *receiver*. The sender can transmit the message verbally, through facial expression, and via body language—and often by a combination of these. Once the message is sent, the receiver must try to determine the meaning of the message. A receiver who fails to attend or listen will miss part, if not all, of the message.

## How Can I Send More Effective Messages?

Young athletes often have little understanding of the rules and skills of baseball, and probably have even less confidence in playing it. So they need accurate, understandable, and supportive messages to help them along. That's why your verbal and nonverbal messages are so important.

### Verbal Messages

"Sticks and stones may break my bones, but words will never hurt me" isn't true. Spoken words can have a strong and long-lasting effect. And coaches' words are particularly influential, because youngsters place great importance on what coaches say. Therefore, whether you are correcting a misbehavior, teaching a player how to field ground balls, or praising a player for good effort,

- *be positive, but honest;*
- *state it clearly and simply;*
- *say it loud enough and say it again; and*
- *be consistent.*

### Be Positive, But Honest

Nothing turns people off like hearing someone nag all the time. Young athletes are similarly discouraged by a coach who gripes constantly. The kids on your team need encouragement, because many of them doubt

their ability to play baseball. So *look* for what your players did well and *tell* them about it.

But don't cover up poor or incorrect play with rosy words of praise. Kids know all too well when they've made a mistake, and no cheerfully expressed cliche can undo their error. And if you fail to acknowledge players' errors, your players will think you are a phony.

A good way to handle situations in which you have identified and must correct improper technique is to serve your players a "compliment sandwich."

1. Point out what the athlete did correctly.
2. Let the player know what was incorrect in the performance and instruct him or her how to correct it.
3. Encourage the player by reemphasizing what he or she did well.

### State It Clearly and Simply

Positive and honest messages are good, but only if expressed directly and in words your players understand. "Beating around the bush" is ineffective and inefficient. If you ramble, your players will miss the point of your message and probably lose interest. Here are some tips for saying things clearly:

- Organize your thoughts before speaking to your athletes.
- Explain things thoroughly, but don't bore them with long-winded monologues.
- Use language that your players can understand. However, avoid trying to be "hip" by using their age group's slang words.

### Say It Loud Enough and Say It Again

A baseball field with kids spread out from deep center field to home plate can make communication difficult. So talk to your team in a voice that all members can hear and interpret. It's okay, in fact appropriate, to soften your voice when speaking to a player individually about a personal problem. But most of the time your messages will be for all your players to hear, so make sure they can! A word of caution, however: Don't dominate the setting with a booming voice that detracts attention from players' performances.

Sometimes what you say, even if stated loud and clear, won't sink in the first time. This may be particularly true with young athletes hearing words they don't understand. To avoid boring repetition but to still get your message across, say the same thing in a slightly different way. For instance, you might first tell your players, "Go to second on a grounder." Then, soon thereafter, re-

mind them, "Throw the ball to second base for a force-out if the ball is hit on the ground to you." The second message may get through to some players who missed it the first time around.

If you still aren't certain whether your players understand, ask them to repeat the message back to you. As the old saying goes, "If they can't say it, they can't play it."

### Be Consistent

People often say something in a way that implies a different message from their words. For example, a sarcastic tone added to the words "way to go" sends an entirely different message than the words themselves suggest. It is essential that you avoid sending such mixed messages. Keep the tone of your voice consistent with the words you use. And don't say something one day and contradict it the next; players will get confused.

## Nonverbal Messages

Just as you should be consistent in the tone of voice and words you use, you should also keep your verbal and nonverbal messages consistent. An extreme example of failing to do this would be shaking your head, indicating disapproval, while at the same time telling a player, "Nice try." Which is the player to believe, your gesture or your words?

Messages can be sent nonverbally in a number of ways. Facial expressions and body language are just two of the more obvious forms of nonverbal signals that can help you when you coach.

### Facial Expressions

The look on a person's face is the quickest clue to what she or he thinks or feels. Your players know this, so they will study your face, looking for any sign that will tell them more than your words. Don't try to fool them by putting on a happy or blank "mask." They'll see through it, and you'll lose credibility.

Serious, stone-faced expressions are also no help to kids who need cues as to how they are performing. They will just assume you're unhappy or disinterested.

So don't be afraid to smile. A smile from a coach can boost the confidence of an unsure young athlete. Plus, a smile lets your players know that you are happy coaching them. But don't overdo it or else your players won't be able to tell when you are genuinely pleased by something they've done or when you are just "putting on" a smiling face.

### Body Language

How would your players think you felt if you came to practice slouched over, with head down and shoulders slumped? Tired? Bored? Unhappy? How would they think you felt if you watched them during a contest with your hands on your hips, jaws clenched, and face reddened? Upset with them? Disgusted at an umpire? Mad at a fan?

Probably some or all of these things would enter your players' minds. That's why you should carry yourself in a pleasant, confident, and vigorous manner. Such a posture not only projects happiness with your coaching role, it also provides a good example for young players who may model your behavior.

Physical contact can also be a very important use of body language. A handshake, a pat on the head, an arm around the shoulder, or even a big hug are effective ways of showing approval, concern, affection, and joy to your players. Youngsters are especially in need of this type of nonverbal message. Keep within the obvious moral and legal limits, but don't be reluctant to touch your players and send a message that can only truly be expressed in that way.

## How Can I Improve My Receiving Skills?

Now let's examine the other half of the communication process—receiving messages. Too often people are very good senders and very poor receivers of messages; they seem to naturally enjoy hearing themselves talk more than listening to others. As a coach of young athletes it is essential that you receive their verbal and nonverbal messages effectively.

You can be a better receiver of your players' messages if you are willing to learn the keys to receiving messages and then make a strong effort to use them with your players. You'll be surprised what you've been missing.

### Attention!

First you must pay attention; you must want to hear what others are communicating to you. That's not always easy when you're busy coaching and have many things competing for your attention. But in one-to-one and team meetings with players, you must really focus on what they are telling you, both verbally and nonverbally. Not only will such focused attention help you catch every word they say, but you'll also notice their mood and physical state, and you'll get an idea of their feelings toward you and other players on the team.

### Listen CARE-FULLY

How we receive messages from others, perhaps more than anything else we do, demonstrates how much we care for the sender and what that person has to tell us. If you care little for your players or have little regard for what they have to say, it will show in how you attend and listen to them.

Check yourself. Do you find your mind wandering while one of your players is talking to you? Do you frequently have to ask, "What did you say?" If so, you need to work on your attending and listening skills. If you find that you're missing the messages your players send, perhaps the most critical question you should ask yourself is this: Do I care?

## How Do I Put It All Together?

So far we've discussed separately the sending and receiving of messages. But we all know that senders and receivers switch roles several times during an interaction. One person initiates a communication by sending a message to another person who receives the message. The receiver then switches roles and becomes the sender by responding to the person who sent the initial message. These verbal and nonverbal responses are called *feedback*.

Your players will be looking to you for feedback all the time. They will want to know how you think they are performing, what you think of their ideas, and whether their efforts please you. *How you respond* will strongly affect your players. So let's take

a look at a few general types of feedback and examine their possible effects.

## Providing Instructions

With young players, much of your feedback will involve answering questions about how to play baseball. Your instructive responses to these questions should include both verbal and nonverbal feedback. Here are suggestions for giving instructional feedback:

- Keep verbal instructions simple and concise.
- Use demonstrations to provide nonverbal instructional feedback (see Unit 4).
- "Walk" players through the skill, or use a slow-motion demonstration if they are having trouble learning.

## Correcting Errors

When your players perform incorrectly, you need to provide informative feedback to correct the error—and the sooner the better. And when you do correct errors, keep in mind these two principles: Use negative criticism sparingly, and keep calm.

### Use Negative Criticism Sparingly

Although you may need to punish players for horseplay or dangerous activities by scolding or temporarily removing them from activity, avoid reprimanding players for performance errors. Admonishing players for honest mistakes makes them afraid to even try; nothing ruins a youngster's enjoyment of a sport more than a coach who harps on every miscue. So instead, correct your players by using the positive approach. They'll enjoy playing more, and you'll enjoy coaching more.

### Keep Calm

Don't fly off the handle when your players make mistakes. Remember, you're coaching young and inexperienced players, not pros. Therefore, you'll see more incorrect than correct technique, and probably have more discipline problems than you expect. But throwing a tantrum over each error or misbehavior will only inhibit your players or suggest to them the wrong kind of behavior to model. So let your players know that mistakes aren't the end of the world; stay cool!

## Positive Feedback

Praising players when they have performed or behaved well is an effective way of getting them to repeat (or try to repeat) that behavior in the future. And positive feedback for effort is an especially effective way to motivate youngsters to work on difficult skills. So rather than shouting and providing negative feedback to a player who has made a mistake, try offering a compliment sandwich, described on page 12.

Sometimes just the way you word feedback can make it more positive than negative. For example, instead of saying, "Don't catch the ball that way," you might say, "Catch the ball this way." Then your players will be focusing on what to *do* instead of what *not* to do.

You can give positive feedback verbally and nonverbally. Telling a player, especially in front of teammates, that he or she has performed well is a great way to increase a kid's confidence. And a pat on the back or

a handshake can be a very tangible way of communicating your recognition of a player's performance.

## Whom Else Do I Need to Communicate With?

Coaching involves not only sending and receiving messages and providing proper feedback to players, but also includes interacting with players' parents, as well as fans, umpires, and opposing coaches. So try these suggestions for communicating with each group.

Coaches, be positive!

Only a very small percentage of ACEP-trained coaches' behaviors are negative.

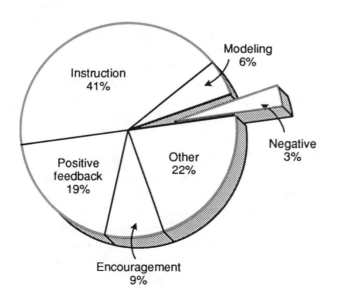

Instruction 41%

Modeling 6%

Negative 3%

Other 22%

Positive feedback 19%

Encouragement 9%

## Parents

A player's parents need to be assured that their daughter or son is under the direction of a coach who is both knowledgeable about baseball and concerned about the youngster's well-being. You can put their worries to rest by holding a preseason parent orientation meeting in which you describe your background and your approach to coaching.

If parents contact you with a concern during the season, listen to them closely and try to offer positive responses. If you need to communicate with parents, catch them after a practice, give them a phone call, or send a note through the mail. Messages sent to parents through children are too often lost, misinterpreted, or forgotten.

## Fans

The stands probably won't be overflowing at your games, but that only means that you'll more easily hear the one or two fans who criticize your coaching. When you hear something negative said about the job you're doing, don't respond. Keep calm, consider whether the message had any value, and if not, forget it. The best approach is to put away your "rabbit ears" and communicate through your actions that you are a confident, competent coach.

Even if you are ready to withstand the negative comments of fans, your players may not be. Prepare them. Tell them that it is you, not the spectators, to whom they should listen. If you notice that one of your players is rattled by a fan's comment, reassure the player that your evaluation is more objective and favorable—and the one that counts.

## Umpires

How you communicate with umpires will have a great influence on the way your players behave toward them. Set an example —greet umpires with a handshake, an introduction, and perhaps some casual conversation about the upcoming contest. Express your respect for them before, during, and after each game.

Keep in mind that most youth baseball umpires are volunteers or are working for a nominal fee. So don't make nasty remarks, shout, or use disrespectful body gestures. Your players will see you do it, and they'll get the idea that such behavior is appropriate. Plus, if the umpire hears or sees you, the communication between the two of you will break down. In short, you take care of the coaching, and let the umpires take care of the umpiring.

## Opposing Coaches

Make an effort to visit with the coach of the opposing team before the game. Perhaps the two of you can work out a special arrangement for the contest, such as allowing players to reenter the game after being replaced in the lineup. During the game, don't get into personal feuds with the opposing coach. Remember, it's the kids, not the coaches, who are competing.

## Summary Checklist

Check your coaching communication skills by answering yes or no to the following questions.

|  | *Yes* | *No* |
|---|---|---|
| 1. Are your verbal messages to your players positive and honest? | ___ | ___ |
| 2. Do you speak loudly, clearly, and in a language your athletes understand? | ___ | ___ |
| 3. Do you remember to repeat instructions to your players, in case they didn't hear you the first time? | ___ | ___ |
| 4. Are your tone of voice and your nonverbal messages consistent with the words you use? | ___ | ___ |
| 5. Do your facial expressions and body language express interest in and happiness with your coaching role? | ___ | ___ |
| 6. Are you attentive to your players and able to pick up even their small verbal and nonverbal cues? | ___ | ___ |
| 7. Do you really care about what your athletes say to you? | ___ | ___ |
| 8. Do you instruct rather than criticize when your players make errors? | ___ | ___ |

|  | Yes | No |
|---|---|---|
| 9. Are you usually positive when responding to what your athletes say and do? | ___ | ___ |
| 10. Do you try to communicate in a cooperative and respectful manner with parents, fans, umpires, and opposing coaches? | ___ | ___ |

If you answered no to any question, you may want to refer back to the section in this chapter where the topic was discussed. *Now* is the time to address communication problems, not when you're on the diamond with your players.

# UNIT 4

# How Do I Get My Team Ready to Play?

To coach baseball, you must understand its basic rules, skills, and strategies. The second part of this *Rookie Coaches Baseball Guide* provides the basic information you'll need to comprehend the sport.

But all the baseball knowledge in the world will do you little good unless you present it effectively to your players. That's why this unit is so important. In it you learn the steps to take in teaching sport skills, as well as practical guidelines for planning your season and individual practices.

## How Do I Teach Baseball Skills?

Many people believe that the only qualification needed to coach is to have played the sport. It's helpful to have played, but there is much more to coaching successfully. And even if you haven't played baseball, you can still teach the skills of the game effectively using this IDEA:

I—Introduce the skill.

D—Demonstrate the skill.

E—Explain the skill.

A—Attend to players practicing the skill.

## Introduce the Skill

Players, especially young and inexperienced ones, need to know what skill they are learning and why they are learning it. You should, therefore, take these three steps every time you introduce a skill to your players:

1. Get your players' attention.
2. Name the skill.
3. Explain the importance of the skill.

### Get Your Players' Attention

Because youngsters are easily distracted, use some method to get their attention. Some coaches use interesting news items or stories. Others use jokes. And others simply project an enthusiasm that gets their players to listen. Whatever method you use, speak slightly above the normal volume and look your players in the eye when you speak.

It helps if you arrange the players in two or three evenly spaced rows, facing you and not some source of distraction (an outfield wall background is recommended). Then check that all can see and hear you before you begin.

### Name the Skill

Although you might mention other common names for the skill, decide which one you'll use and stick with it. This will help avoid confusion and enhance communication among your players. For example, choose either "bunt" or "lay it down" as the term for the appropriate offensive skill, and use it consistently.

### Explain the Importance of the Skill

Although the importance of a skill may be apparent to you, your players may be less able to see how the skill will help them become better baseball players. Offer them a reason for learning the skill and describe how it relates to more advanced skills. For instance, explain that the bunt is an effective tool for getting a hit against difficult pitchers and for moving base runners. Then explain that the bunt can be used as a surprise tactic against teams who are looking for a hitter to swing away.

## Demonstrate the Skill

Demonstration is the most important part of teaching a baseball skill to young players who may have never done anything that resembles it. They need a picture, not just words. They need to *see* how the skill is performed.

If you are unable to perform the skill correctly, have an assistant coach or someone skilled in baseball perform the demonstration. A high school varsity player would be an excellent choice. These tips will help make your demonstrations more effective:

- Use correct form.
- Demonstrate the skill several times.
- Slow down the skill, if possible, during one or two performances so players can see every movement involved.
- Perform the skill at different angles so your players can get a full perspective of it.
- Demonstrate the skill with both the right and left hand.

---

*The most difficult aspect of coaching is this: Coaches must learn to let athletes learn. Sport skills should be taught so they have meaning to the child, not just meaning to the coach.*

Rainer Martens, ACEP Founder

---

## Explain the Skill

Players learn more effectively when they're given a brief explanation of the skill along with the demonstration. Use simple terms to describe the skill and, if possible, relate it to previously learned skills. Ask your players if they understand your description. If one of them looks confused, have her or him explain the skill back to you.

Complex skills often are better understood if they are explained in more manageable parts. For instance, if you want to teach your players how to field ground balls in the infield, you might take the following steps:

1. Show them a correct performance of the entire skill and explain its function in baseball.

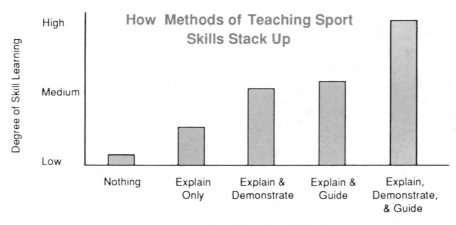

As you observe players' efforts in drills and activities, offer positive, corrective feedback in the form of the "compliment sandwich" described in Unit 3. If a player performs the skill properly, acknowledge it and offer praise. Keep in mind that your feedback will have a great influence on your players' motivation to practice and improve their skills.

Remember, too, that young players need individual instruction. So set aside a time before, during, or after practice to give them individual help.

2. Break down the skill and point out its component parts to your players.
3. Have players perform each of the component skills you have already taught them, such as getting into the ready position, sliding or charging to meet the ball, looking it into the glove, stopping, pivoting, and throwing to the appropriate base.
4. After players have demonstrated their ability to perform the separate parts of the skill in sequence, reexplain the entire skill.
5. Have them practice the skill.

## Attend to Players Practicing the Skill

If the skill you selected was within your players' capabilities and you have done an effective job of introducing, demonstrating, and explaining, your players should be ready to attempt it. Some players may need to be physically guided through the movements during their first few tries.

For example, some players may need your hands-on help to grip the bat and position their arms properly on their initial hitting attempts. Walking unsure athletes through the skill in this way will help them gain confidence to perform the skill on their own.

Your teaching duties don't end when all your athletes have demonstrated that they understand how to perform the skill. In fact, a significant part of your teaching will involve observing closely the hit-and-miss trial performances of your players.

## What Planning Do I Need to Do?

Beginning coaches often make the mistake of showing up for the first practice with no particular plan in mind. These coaches find that their practices are unorganized, that their players are frustrated and inattentive, and that the amount and quality of their skill instruction is limited. Planning is essential to successful teaching *and* coaching. And it doesn't begin on the way to practice!

## Preseason Planning

Effective coaches begin planning well before the start of the season. Here are preseason measures that will make the season more enjoyable, successful, and safe for you and your players:

• Become familiar with the sport organization you are involved in, especially its

You may be surprised at the number of things you should do even before the first practice. But if you address them during the preseason, the season will be much more enjoyable and productive for you and your players.

## In-Season Planning

Your choice of activities during the season should teach your players physical and mental skills, a knowledge of rules and game tactics, sportsmanship, and a love for the sport. All of these goals are important, but we'll focus on the skills and tactics of baseball to help you itemize your objectives.

### Goal Setting

What you plan to do during the season must be reasonable for the maturity and skill level of your players. In terms of baseball skills and tactics, you should teach young players the basics and move on to more complex activities only after they have mastered these easier techniques and strategies.

To begin the season, your instructional goals might include the following:

- Players will be able to get into the ready position in the field.
- Players will be able to assume an effective stance when batting.
- Players will be able to grip the ball for proper release.
- Players will be able to throw the ball to a target.
- Players will be able to use proper mechanics when catching the ball.
- Players will demonstrate knowledge of baseball rules.
- Players will demonstrate knowledge of basic offensive and defensive strategies.
- Players will be able to communicate with teammates.
- Players will develop a respect for teamwork.
- Players will play hard and have fun at the same time.
- Players will show respect for umpires, coaches, and other players.
- Players will learn how to win with class and how to lose with grace.

philosophy and goals regarding youth sport.
- Examine the availability of facilities, equipment, instructional aids, and other materials needed for practices and games.
- Check to see if you have liability insurance to cover you if one of your players is hurt. If you don't, get some.
- Establish your coaching priorities regarding having fun, developing players' skills, and winning.
- Select and meet with your assistant coaches to discuss the philosophy, goals, team rules, and plans for the season.
- Register players for the team. Have them complete a player information form and obtain medical clearance forms, if required.
- Institute an injury-prevention program for your players.
- Hold a parent orientation meeting to inform parents of your background, philosophy, goals, and instructional approach. Also, give a brief overview of the league's rules and baseball rules, terms, and strategies to familiarize parents or guardians with the sport.

### Organizing

After you've defined the skills and tactics you want your players to learn during the season, you can plan how to teach them to your players in practices. But be flexible! If your players are having difficulty learning a skill or tactic, take some extra time until they get the hang of it—even if that means moving back your schedule. After all, if your players can't perform the fundamental skills, they'll never execute the more complex skills you have scheduled for them.

Still, it helps to have a plan for progressing players through skills during the season. The sample 8-week season plan in the appendix shows how to schedule your skill instruction in an organized and progressive manner. If this is your first coaching experience, you may wish to follow the plan as it stands. If you have some previous experience, you may want to modify the schedule to better fit the needs of your team.

## What Makes Up a Good Practice?

A good instructional plan makes practice preparation much easier. Have players work on more important and less difficult goals in early season practice sessions. And see to it that players master basic skills before moving on to more advanced ones.

It is helpful to establish *one objective* for each practice, but try to include a *variety of activities* related to that objective. This can make an otherwise boring baseball practice fun. For example, although your primary objective might be to improve players' fly ball catching skill, you should have players perform several different drills designed to enhance that single skill. And to interject further variety into your practices, vary the order of scheduled activities.

In general, we recommend that each of your practices include the following:

- *Warm up*
- *Practice previously taught skills*
- *Teach and practice new skills*
- *Practice under gamelike conditions*
- *Cool down*
- *Evaluate*

### Warm Up

As you're checking the roster and announcing the performance objectives for the practice, your players should be preparing their bodies for vigorous activity. A 5- to 10-minute period of easy-paced activities (e.g., three-quarter-speed running around the field), stretching, and calisthenics should be sufficient for youngsters to limber their muscles and reduce the risk of injury.

### Practice Previously Taught Skills

Devote part of each practice to working on the fundamental skills players already know. But remember, kids like variety. So organize and modify drills to keep everyone involved and interested. Praise and encourage players when you notice improvement, and offer individual assistance to those who need help.

### Teach and Practice New Skills

Gradually build on your players' existing skills by giving them something new to practice each session. The proper method for teaching sport skills is described on pages 19 to 21. Refer to those pages if you have any questions about teaching new skills or if you want to evaluate your teaching approach periodically during the season.

## Practice Under Gamelike Conditions

Competition among teammates during practices prepares players for actual games and informs young athletes about their abilities relative to those of their peers. Youngsters also seem to have more fun in competitive activities.

You can create contest-like conditions by using competitive drills, modified games, and scrimmages (see Units 7 and 8). However, consider the following guidelines before introducing competition into your practices:

- All players should have an equal opportunity to participate.
- Match players by ability and physical maturity.
- Make sure players can execute fundamental skills before they compete in groups.
- Emphasize performing well, not winning, in every competition.
- Give players room to make mistakes by avoiding constant evaluation of their performances.

## Cool Down

Each practice should wind down with a 5- to 10-minute period of light exercise, including jogging, performance of simple skills, and some stretching. The cool-down allows athletes' bodies to return to the resting state and avoid stiffness, and affords you an opportunity to review the practice.

## Evaluate

At the end of practice spend a few minutes with your players reviewing how well the session accomplished the objective you had set. Even if your evaluation is negative, show optimism for future practices and send players off on an upbeat note.

## How Do I Put a Practice Together?

Simply knowing the six practice components is not enough. You must also be able to arrange those components into a logical progression and fit them into a time schedule. Now, using your instructional goals as a guide for selecting what skills to have your players work on, try to plan several sample baseball practices. The sample practice plan on page 25 should help you get started.

## Summary Checklist

During your baseball season, check your teaching and planning skills periodically. As you gain more coaching experience, you should be able to answer yes to each of the following:

*When you teach baseball skills to your players, do you*

- \_\_\_\_ arrange the players so all can see and hear?
- \_\_\_\_ introduce the skill clearly and explain its importance?
- \_\_\_\_ demonstrate the skill properly several times?
- \_\_\_\_ explain the skill simply and accurately?
- \_\_\_\_ attend closely to players practicing the skill?
- \_\_\_\_ offer corrective, positive feedback or praise after observing players' attempts at the skill?

*When you plan, do you remember to plan for*

____ preseason events like player registration, liability protection, use of facilities, and parent orientation?
____ season goals such as the development of players' physical skills, mental skills, sportsmanship, and enjoyment?
____ practice components such as warmup, practicing previously taught skills, teaching and practicing new skills, practicing under gamelike conditions, cool-down, and evaluation?

## Sample Practice Plan

*Performance Objective.* Players will be able to use proper technique when catching a ball.

| Component | Time | Activity or drill |
| --- | --- | --- |
| Warm up | 10 min | Easy running—400 yards<br>Stretching (see Unit 5)<br>Pickups |
| Practice previously taught skills | 25 min | Fielding drills, such as the Short Hop Drill (see Unit 7) |
| Teach and practice new skills | 15 min | Positioning to field balls hit in the air and on the ground |
| Practice under gamelike conditions | 20 min | |
| Cool down and evaluate | 10 min | Easy jogging<br>Stretching<br>Quick review<br>Reminder about next practice |

# What Can I Do for Safety?

One of your players rounds third and heads for home plate. The throw from the outfield arrives at home just ahead of the runner. Sliding to avoid the tag, your player catches a leg on one of the catcher's shin guards. The runner is called "safe" by the umpire, but he is not getting up and seems to be in pain. What do you do?

One of the unpleasant aspects of coaching is seeing players get hurt. Fortunately, there are many preventive measures coaches can institute to reduce the risk. But in spite of such efforts, injury re-

mains a reality of sport participation. Consequently, you must be prepared to provide first aid when injuries occur and to protect yourself against unjustified lawsuits. This unit will describe how you can

• create the safest possible environment for your players,

- provide emergency first aid to players when they get hurt, and
- protect yourself from injury liability.

## How Do I Keep My Players From Getting Hurt?

Injuries may occur because of poor preventive measures. Part of your planning, described in Unit 4, should include steps that give your players the best possible chance for injury-free participation. These steps include the following:

- *Preseason physical examination*
- *Physical conditioning*
- *Equipment and facilities inspection*
- *Matching players by physical maturity and warning of inherent risks*
- *Liability waivers*
- *Proper supervision and record keeping*
- *Sufficient hydration*
- *Warm-up and cool-down*

## Preseason Physical Examination

Even in the absence of severe injury or ongoing illness, your players should have a physical examination every 2 years. Any player with a known complication should obtain a physician's consent before participation is allowed. You should also have players' parents or guardians sign a participation agreement and a release form to allow their daughter or son to be treated in case of an emergency.

## Physical Conditioning

Muscles, tendons, and ligaments unaccustomed to vigorous and long-lasting physical activity are prone to injury. Therefore, prepare your athletes to withstand the exertion of playing baseball. An effective conditioning program would include running and throwing.

Make conditioning drills and activities fun. Include a skill component such as baserunning to prevent players from becoming

---

**Informed Consent Form**

I hereby give my permission for _____ to participate in

_____ during the athletic season beginning in 199____. Further, I authorize the school to provide emergency treatment of an injury to or illness of my child if qualified medical personnel consider treatment necessary *and* perform the treatment. This authorization is granted only if I cannot be reached and a reasonable effort has been made to do so.

Date _____     Parent or guardian _____

Address _____     Phone ( ___ ) _____

Family physician _____     Phone ( ___ ) _____

Pre-existing medical conditions (e.g., allergies or chronic illnesses) _____

_____

Other(s) to also contact in case of emergency _____

Relationship to child _____     Phone ( ___ ) _____

My child and I are aware that participating in _____ is a potentially hazardous activity. I assume all risks associated with participation in this sport, including but not limited to falls, contact with other participants, the effects of the weather, traffic, and other reasonable risk conditions associated with the sport. All such risks to my child are known and understood by me.

I understand this informed consent form and agree to its conditions on behalf of my child.

Child's signature _____     Date _____

Parent's signature _____     Date _____

bored or looking upon the activity as "work."

## Equipment and Facilities Inspection

Another means to prevent injuries is to check the quality and fit of the clothes worn by your players. Slick-soled, poor-fitting, or unlaced baseball shoes; unstrapped eyeglasses; and jewelry are dangerous on the baseball diamond. Specify to players what they should wear. Shorts are out if they are going to be sliding; rubber-studded cleats are essential for good footing.

Remember to examine regularly the field on which your players practice and play. Remove hazards, report conditions you cannot remedy, and request maintenance as necessary.

## Matching Athletes by Maturity and Warning of Inherent Risks

Children of the same age may differ in height and weight by as much as 6 inches and 50 pounds. In baseball, size is less of an advantage than in some other sports. Yet it is hardly fair to pit an underdeveloped young athlete against a tall, strong, smoke-throwing pitcher. Try to give smaller, less mature children a better chance to succeed

and avoid injury, and larger children more of a challenge. Experience, ability, and emotional maturity are additional factors to keep in mind when matching players on the field.

Matching helps protect you from certain liability concerns. But you also must warn players of the inherent risks involved in playing baseball, because "failure to warn" is one of the most successful arguments in lawsuits against coaches. So thoroughly explain the inherent risks of baseball and make sure each player and his or her parent or guardian know, understand, and appreciate those risks.

## Liability Waivers

The preseason parent orientation meeting is a good opportunity to explain the risks of the sport to parents and players. It is also a good occasion to have both the players and their parents sign waivers releasing you from liability should an injury occur. Such waivers do not discharge you of responsibility for your players' well-being, but they are recommended by lawyers.

## Proper Supervision and Record Keeping

When you work with youngsters, your mere presence in the area of play is not enough; you must actively plan and direct team activities and closely observe and evaluate players' participation. You're the watchdog responsible for their welfare. So if you notice a player limping or grimacing, give her or him a rest, and examine the extent of the injury.

As a coach, you're also required to enforce the rules of the sport, prohibit dangerous horseplay, and hold practices only under safe weather conditions. These specific supervisory activities will make the play environment safer for your players and help protect you from liability should an injury occur.

For further protection, keep records of your season plans, practice plans, and any player injuries. Season and practice plans come in handy if you need evidence that players have been taught certain skills, and accurate, detailed accident reports offer protection against unfounded lawsuits. Ask for these forms from the organization to which you belong. And hold onto such records for several years so an "old baseball injury" of a former player doesn't come back to haunt you.

## Sufficient Hydration

You know how hot and humid it can get out on a baseball field at the height of summer. And if you add to that a lot of activity and competition, body temperatures can really rise. So baseball players need a ready supply of cool water to keep from dehydrating. And they may need a reminder from you to take a water break, because by the time they are aware of their thirst, they are long overdue for a drink.

## Warm-Up and Cool-Down

Although young bodies are generally very limber, they also can get tight from inactivity, so a warm-up of about 10 minutes before each practice is strongly recommended. The warm-up should address each muscle group and elevate the heart rate in preparation for strenuous activity. Easy running followed by these stretching exercises is a common sequence (hold each stretch for 20 seconds, then release):

**Side and Shoulder Stretch**—Stand with one arm extended straight up, then tilt the upper body to the opposite side, reaching the hand up and across. Repeat the stretch on the other side. For the shoulder stretch, extend one arm across the chest, grasp the raised elbow with the opposite hand, and pull the elbow toward the body (see Figure 5.1). Repeat the stretch on the other side.

**Triceps Stretch**—Sit or stand upright with one arm flexed and raised overhead next to your ear, and your hand resting on your shoulder blade. Grasp your elbow with the opposite hand and pull your elbow behind your head. Switch arms and repeat the stretch.

**Figure 5.1**   The shoulder stretch.

**Ankle Stretch**—Sit upright on the ground with one leg crossed over the opposite knee. Grasp your ankle and the heel of your foot with one hand, and the top outside portion of your foot with the other hand. Slowly turn your ankle inward, hold the stretch, and relax. Switch legs and repeat the stretch.

**Achilles Tendon Stretch**—Stand upright 4 or 5 steps from a fence. Bend one leg and place it forward, keep your opposite leg straight, and lean against the fence without losing the straight line of your head, neck, spine, pelvis, outstretched leg, and ankle (see Figure 5.2). Keep your rear foot down, flat, and straight ahead. Bend your arms, move your chest toward the wall, and shift your weight forward. Switch legs and repeat the stretch.

**Figure 5.2**   The Achilles tendon stretch.

**Hip Flexor Stretch**—Stand upright, flex one knee, and roll the opposite foot under so the top of the instep rests on the floor. Placing your hands on your hips and keeping the chest and shoulders upright, press your hips toward the ground. Repeat the stretch on the other side (see Figure 5.3).

**Figure 5.3**   The hip flexor stretch.

**Hamstring Stretch**—Sit upright on the ground. Flex one knee and slide that heel toward your groin so that the heel is against the inner side of your opposite thigh. A 90-degree angle should be formed between your extended leg and flexed leg. Keeping the extended leg straight, bend at the waist and lower the torso toward the straight leg (see Figure 5.4). Switch legs and repeat the stretch.

**Figure 5.4**   The hamstring stretch.

**Lower Back Stretch**—Lie flat on your back with your arms by your hips, palms down. Push down on the ground with your palms, raise your legs to a vertical position, and support your body with your hands placed under your lower back.

**Charley Horse Stretch**—Lie on your stomach. Bend one knee and try to touch that heel to the buttock. Next, grasp that

ankle with the same-side hand. Slowly pull your ankle toward the back of your head (see Figure 5.5). Avoid twisting your trunk. Switch legs and repeat the stretch.

**Figure 5.5**   The charley horse stretch.

As practice is winding down, slow players' heart rate with an easy jog or walk. Then arrange for a 5- or 10-minute period of easy stretching at the end of practice to help players avoid stiff muscles and make them less tight before the next practice.

## What If One of My Players Gets Hurt?

No matter how thorough your prevention program, injuries will occur. And when injury does strike, chances are you will be the one in charge. The severity and nature of the injury will determine how actively involved you'll be in treating the injury. But regardless of how seriously a player is hurt, it is your responsibility to know what steps to take. So let's look at how you can provide *basic* emergency care to your injured athletes.

---

### ACEP Fact

Reports of injury rates for youth baseball range from 2% to 10%.

---

### Minor Injuries

Although no injury seems minor to the person experiencing it, most injuries are neither life-threatening nor severe enough to restrict participation. And if such an injury occurs, you can take an active role in the initial treatment.

### Scrapes and Cuts

When a player has an open wound, first put on a pair of disposable surgical gloves or some other effective blood barrier. Then follow these three steps:

1. Stop the bleeding by applying direct pressure with a clean dressing to the wound and elevating it. *Do not* remove the dressing if it becomes blood-soaked. Instead, place an additional dressing on top of the one already in place. If bleeding continues, elevate the injured area above the heart and maintain pressure. Then have the player receive trained medical attention.

2. Cleanse the wound thoroughly once the bleeding is controlled. A good rinsing with a forceful stream of water, and perhaps light scrubbing with soap, will help prevent infection.

3. Protect the wound with sterile gauze or a bandage. If the player continues to participate, apply protective padding over the injured area.

For bloody noses not associated with serious facial injury, have the athlete sit and lean slightly forward. Then pinch the player's nostrils shut. If the bleeding continues after several minutes or if the athlete has a history of nosebleeds, seek medical assistance.

### Sprains and Strains

The physical demands of baseball practices and games often result in injury to the muscles or tendons (strains), and sometimes to the ligaments (sprains). When your players suffer minor strains or sprains, immediately apply the RICE method of injury care.

---

**ACEP Fact**

Approximately half of all youth pitchers report experiencing elbow pain.

---

### Bumps and Bruises

Inevitably, baseball players make contact with each other and with the ground. And if the force of a body part at impact is great enough, a bump or bruise will result. Many players will continue playing with such sore spots. But if the bump or bruise is large and painful, you should act appropriately. Enact the RICE formula for injury care and monitor the injury. If swelling, discoloration, and

---

## The RICE Method

**R**—Rest the area to avoid further damage and foster healing.

**I**—Ice the area to reduce swelling and pain.

**C**—Compress the area by securing an ice bag in place with an elastic wrap.

**E**—Elevate the injury above heart level to keep the blood from pooling in the area.

pain have lessened, the player may resume participation with protective padding; if not, the player should be examined by a physician.

## Serious Injuries

Head and spine injuries, fractures, and injuries that cause a player to lose consciousness are among a class of injuries that you cannot and *should not try to treat* yourself. But *you should plan* what you'll do if such an injury occurs. And your plan should include the following guidelines for action:

- Obtain the phone number and ensure the availability of nearby emergency care units.
- Assign an assistant coach or another *adult* the responsibility of contacting emergency medical help upon your request.
- Do *not move* the injured athlete.
- Calm the injured athlete and keep others away from him or her as much as possible.
- Evaluate whether the athlete's breathing is stopped or irregular and, if necessary, clear the airway with your fingers.
- Administer artificial respiration if breathing has stopped.
- Administer cardiopulmonary resuscitation (CPR), or have a trained individual administer CPR, if the athlete's circulation has stopped.
- Remain with the athlete until medical personnel arrive.

## How Do I Protect Myself?

When one of your players is injured, naturally your first concern is his or her well-being. Your feelings for children, after all, are what made you decide to coach. Unfortunately, there is something else that you must consider: Can you be held liable for the injury?

From a legal standpoint, a coach has nine duties to fulfill. In this unit we've discussed all but planning (see Unit 4).

1. Provide a safe environment.
2. Properly plan the activity.
3. Provide adequate and proper equipment.
4. Match athletes by size and maturity.
5. Warn of inherent risks in the sport.
6. Supervise the activity closely.
7. Evaluate athletes for injury or incapacity.
8. Know emergency procedures and first aid.
9. Keep adequate records.

In addition to fulfilling these nine legal duties, you should check your insurance coverage to make sure your present policy will protect you from liability.

## Summary Self-Test

Now that you've read how to make your coaching experience safe for your players and yourself, test your knowledge of the material by answering these questions:

1. What are eight injury prevention measures you can institute to try to keep your players from getting hurt?

2. What is the three-step emergency care process for cuts?

3. What method of treatment is best for minor sprains and strains?

4. What steps can you take to manage serious injuries?

5. What are the nine legal duties of a coach?

# UNIT 6

# *What Do I Need to Know About Baseball?*

America's favorite pastime—this expression captures how tens of millions of baseball fans in the United States feel about their sport. And their love of baseball is shared by millions more fans in Canada, Central America, Cuba, Japan, and elsewhere.

For baseball players and coaches, however, it's not simply a matter of "fun at the ol' ballpark." This may surprise you if you are a beginning coach. But if you've coached baseball before, you realize there's more to it than bringing the bats and balls and filling out the starting lineup.

Whether you are a first-time or veteran youth baseball coach, you are probably interested in teaching the game effectively to young players. The next three units of the *Rookie Coaches Baseball Guide* provide the baseball and T-ball basics you need to do the job. Included are the basic rules, skills, strategies, and drills you and your players should know.

## Coaching Youth Baseball

So why take the time and trouble to coach baseball? Perhaps the best reason is that kids love the sport. Give them a bat and ball and they'll play until it's too dark to see.

---

### ACEP Fact

Baseball is a hit among America's youth—more than 4 million participate in organized youth baseball each year.

---

Kids' fondness for the game, however, is both a plus and a minus when it comes to coaching them. On the plus side, their interest and previous baseball experience should make them eager students of the game. On the minus side, because they have watched the pros, they may think they know more than they actually do about the skills required to play baseball. So don't be shocked if one of your outfielders gets plunked on the head while trying to make a one-handed basket catch; that's part of the learning process, and part of coaching.

But what a great opportunity! Coaching baseball gives you a chance to share with kids your knowledge and love of the game. The first time a player you taught how to swing the bat gets a hit, you'll be hooked.

Your challenge as a youth baseball coach is to instruct your players well in the fundamentals of baseball and to maintain their interest while still allowing them to have fun. To meet this challenge, read the rest of this guide and then take your players to the PARK:

**P**—Prepare to teach proper fundamental skill development.

**A**—Always instill good sportsmanship and respect for the rules.

**R**—Repeat instructions as a key to good teaching.

**K**—Keep it fun!

## What Are the Rules?

Baseball rules vary slightly at the different age levels of participation. The most common modifications involve the size of the diamond (see Figures 6.1-6.4) and the length of the game. Variations of the game, like coach-pitch, machine-pitch, and T-ball, in which players hit a ball off a tee, often use soft-core balls to make the game less threatening to very young players. Your team will probably play by league rules, established nationally for appropriate age-group divisions.

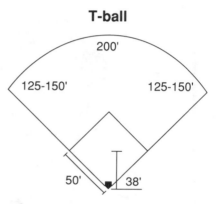

**Figure 6.1** Baseball diamond dimensions for T-ball.

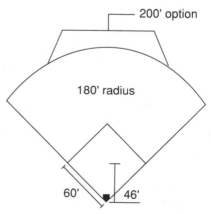

**Figure 6.2** Baseball diamond dimensions for standard youth league (ages 12 and under).

**Modified Intermediate League**

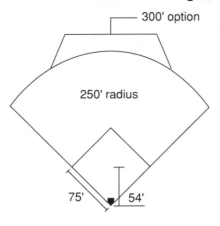

**Figure 6.3** Baseball diamond dimensions for modified intermediate league (optional for ages 14 and under).

**Regulation Field**

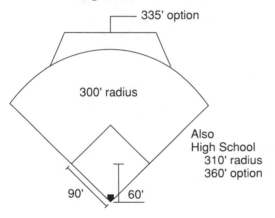

**Figure 6.4** Baseball diamond dimensions for regulation field (ages 13 and above).

## Playing Field

Baseball is played on a diamond-shaped field, with home plate and first, second, and third bases forming the corners. *Foul lines* running from home to first base and third base extend beyond those bases. The area inside the foul lines is *fair territory*, outside is *foul territory*.

Fair territory around the base portion of the field is called the infield. Fair territory in the grassy portion of the field farther from the plate is called the outfield (see Figure 6.5).

## Equipment

You're probably aware of most standard pieces of baseball equipment: bases, ball, bat, gloves, helmets, and other appropriate apparel. But do you know how to tell when this equipment meets proper specifications and is in good repair? Here are some tips.

### Bases

If your league doesn't use breakaway bases, encourage the league office to make this wise investment. Because as many as 70% of baseball injuries occur when players slide, you owe it to youngsters to make the bases as safe as possible.

### Ball

A standard-size baseball is 9 to 9-1/4 inches in circumference and weighs 5 to 5-1/4 ounces. The stitching connecting the two panels of cowhide or horsehide protrudes just enough to allow a player to grip the ball tightly with the fingers. Rubber-coated, softer balls are often used in T-ball and coach-pitch. Using these balls prevents beginning players from developing a fear of catching or fielding the hard-core baseball. Such a fear can impede their skill development.

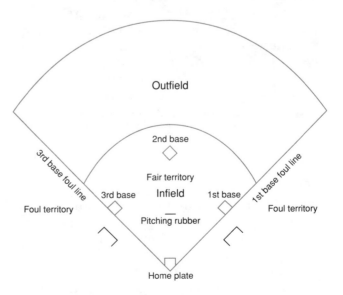

**Figure 6.5** The playing field.

## Bat

The bat is divided into three parts: the knob, the handle, and the barrel (see Figure 6.6).

Knob     Handle                    Barrel

**Figure 6.6**  The baseball bat.

Bats must be all wood or all aluminum. Rubber sheaths are permitted on aluminum bat knobs and handles to improve the grip. Legal aluminum bats are made of one piece and some have a plug in the barrel end. The bat should be light and not long. A bat with a large hitting end tapering down to a small handle gives the greatest center of gravity with which to get the most power on the ball.

---

### Helping Players Select a Bat

Finding bats light enough for young baseball players is no longer a problem with the widespread availability of aluminum bats. Replacing weight as a primary factor in bat selection are length and shape.

Longer bats (32-34 inches) can provide more power through the strike zone, if the hitter is strong enough and can generate great bat speed. Shorter bats (29-31 inches) are best for smaller players who are unable to generate appropriate power.

The handle of the bat should be thin enough for the player to easily grip both hands around. After that, it's up to the players' personal preference what bat they feel most comfortable using.

---

## Glove

No piece of equipment will become more dear to your baseball players than their gloves. So help your players select proper-fitting gloves. It's better to start with a broken-in smaller glove than an oversized one. A mitt that has a huge pocket and is a lot bigger than a youngster's hand will be hard to control and could hinder skill development.

*Breaking in* or conditioning a glove will help create a good pocket and make the glove strong and flexible. Players can rub some hot water or saddle soap into the center of their gloves, stuff a couple of softballs or a large wad of crumpled newspaper into the pocket, and then use shoelaces to tie the glove (see Figure 6.7). Leaving the mitt like this for several days will create a good round pocket. Well-conditioned gloves will improve your players' ability to field and hold onto the ball.

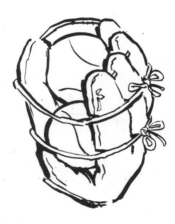

**Figure 6.7**  Tying two softballs in the glove pocket with shoelaces creates a good round pocket.

## Apparel

Helmets and player uniforms are often furnished by the league office. Take time to check the fit and condition of every item of apparel you distribute. All young players should wear baseball shoes with rubber cleats. Double-tying the laces will prevent them from coming untied, which can cause a player to trip. Players should also wear baseball caps to keep the sun out of their eyes.

In addition, some positions require special equipment. The catcher will need a face mask, throat guard, chest protector, and shin guards. And you should encourage all male players, but particularly the catcher, pitcher, and third baseman, to wear a protective cup.

## Game Procedures

At the start of the game, certain procedures are followed to ensure that the game will run smoothly and that coaches on both teams know about any special rules concerning the playing field or boundaries. Here are some common elements of any baseball game:

- Home team is usually predetermined by league officials, but if not, use a coin flip to determine the home team (who bats second).
- Each team has nine players participating in the game at any time. In addition, each team may have one designated hitter, who may substitute at bat for any player in the field.
- A game is divided into innings. Specific youth league rules may determine that a game should be 5, 6, 7, or 9 innings. The most common length of a game is 7 innings.
- The batting order must be followed throughout the game unless a player is substituted for another. Substitutes must take the same place in the batting order as the replaced player.
- Each team gets one turn at bat per inning. Each batter is allowed a maximum of 3 strikes or 4 balls.
- A batter makes an out by striking out (3 strikes), grounding out (the ball touches the ground before being caught and is thrown to first base before the batter arrives), or flying out (the ball is caught by a fielder before it touches the ground).
- A run is scored if an offensive player reaches first, second, and third bases and home plate without being tagged out or forced out (a defensive player with the ball touches the base before the runner arrives; the runner cannot retreat to the previous base because a teammate is already advancing there).
- With the third out, a team's turn at bat ends. That team takes the field, and the opposing team bats.

- The team with the most runs at the end of the game is the winner.
- Extra innings are played to determine the winner of a game tied at the end of regulation play.
- Should rain or inclement weather cause play to be suspended, an official game may be recorded after 5 innings (after 4-1/2 innings if the home team is leading in a scheduled 7-inning contest). Review your league rules. Some may say games are to be played to completion.

### Special Considerations for T-Ball

You might ask how young children play baseball when they can't pitch the ball over the plate nor hit it when they do get a good pitch. They don't. They may play T-ball instead.

T-ball is like baseball, but it is a safer and more enjoyable way for young kids to learn the game. No more wild pitches. No more quaking at the plate. No more 20-walk games. No wonder it's such a popular alternative!

Although it is a modified version of baseball, youngsters playing T-ball consider it just as important. So make sure you treat the game respectfully around your players.

Here are the primary ways in which T-ball differs from baseball:

- Runners must be on the bag when contact is made at the plate.
- Stealing bases is not permitted.
- The play is over when the ball has been returned to the catcher at home plate.
- No balls and strikes are called.
- Hitters must put the ball in play off the tee. The batter is out if she or he fails to put the ball in play after two swinging strikes.

T-ball games could go on forever. Here are a few ideas for structuring a game:

- Set a time limit of 30-40 minutes.
- Let all nine batters hit and then switch sides.
- Play two-out innings.

## Umpires

Umpires are officials who enforce the rules of the game. Youth league games usually have two umpires—one at home plate and another positioned according to the number of base runners and bases that they occupy. Before the game, the umpire meets with both coaches at home plate, where they exchange their lineups. Umpires decide whether a pitch is a ball or a strike, whether a hit is fair or foul, whether a runner is safe or out. The home plate umpire is the ultimate decision-maker on any ruling.

Like you, umpires are volunteers, not professionals. Consequently, from time to time they will make mistakes. How you react when you think an umpire has erred is very important. Be a good role model for your players. If you think a rule was not properly enforced, calmly call *time out* and discuss it with the umpire. Don't mutter about the call in the dugout or interrupt the game by arguing.

## Player Positions

Baseball is played with nine players in the field on defense. Busiest of these nine are the pitcher and catcher, known as the battery. Infielders, who handle ground balls and pop-ups on the dirt portion of the field, include the first baseman, second baseman, shortstop, and third baseman. Covering the outfield are the right fielder, center fielder, and left fielder.

One of your biggest coaching decisions involves answering this question: Who should play which position? Here are some tips to help you choose wisely:

- Put your best defensive players "up the middle" at catcher, pitcher, middle infielders (second base and shortstop), and center fielder.
- Set your lineup to maximize your players' strengths and interests.
- Give your players experience at a variety of positions throughout the season to expand their skills and understanding of the game. You might be surprised when a player exhibits skills at one po-

sition that were not evident at a previous defensive spot.

More specifically, as you determine where on the field each player should play, consider these suggestions about each position.

**Pitcher**—Arm strength or velocity is an indication that a player may make a successful pitcher. A solid mental and emotional makeup will also make a pitcher effective because a pitcher must keep poised throughout the game. Your pitcher should be a tough, smart, and confident competitor who will rise to the occasion when confronting a challenge. Spend a lot of time with your pitchers.

**Catcher**—The catcher is the team's quarterback. All the action takes place in front of this masked player working behind the plate. Good catchers are rugged individuals, and if they are not big and strong, then they must be tough. The position requires strength, endurance, and great hand-eye coordination. The catcher is up and down from a squat position on every pitch, throwing balls back to the pitcher or infielders, backing up first base on all infield ground balls, and chasing short foul balls.

## Infielders

Most balls hit during a youth baseball game don't travel very far. So if your team is going to be successful, you'll need to develop alert and capable infielders. A good infielder must have good hands to catch ground balls, a strong throwing arm (especially the shortstop and third baseman), and quick feet.

The ability to get in front of the ball, field it cleanly, and make an accurate throw requires coordination. Infielders must be able to handle their bodies with ease and think on their feet. With the exception of the pitcher, first baseman, and catcher, infielders should be right-handed. Left-handed infielders have too difficult a throw to make after stopping any ball hit to their right and squaring up to throw.

**First baseman**—The ability to catch thrown balls is most essential for a first baseman. Size, powerful hitting, speed, grace of movement, good fielding of ground balls, and good judgment of infield flies are also qualities of a good first baseman. A strong and accurate arm is a bonus at this position, because of the number of times a first baseman handles the ball. Almost every play is centered around first base.

**Second baseman**—Players of all different statures have become excellent second sackers. Whether big or little, however, a second baseman must have a "sure" pair of hands with which to field ground balls, pop flys, and thrown balls. Moreover, a second baseman must have the ability to foresee fielding situations and act instantly.

**Third baseman**—The third baseman must possess agility, good hands, and quick reflexes. This player must have the ability to come in fast on the ball and throw accurately while running at top speed. She or he must be able to make off-balance throws and bare-hand pick-ups on bunts and slow hit balls. The third baseman must have a strong arm to make the long throws to first base.

**Shortstop**—A shortstop must be alert, be able to start and stop quickly, possess a sure pair of hands, and, above all, have a strong throwing arm. This player must also have quick reactions. The shortstop will be required to make more tough plays than any other player on the field.

## Outfielders

A solid outfield adds to the defensive strength of your team. A good outfielder must be able to run fast, throw far and accurately, judge fly balls, and field ground balls.

**Left fielder**—The left fielder can have less speed and a weaker arm than any other outfielder because many of the throws do not cover a great distance. However, this player must still be alert, have a good arm to the plate, and be a good fielder of ground balls. The left fielder backs up third base whenever necessary.

**Center fielder**—This player must be very fast and have a strong arm. The center fielder covers more territory than any other player and will make the greatest percentage of outfield putouts. The center fielder backs up second base on all sacrifice bunts and on every attempted putout at second.

**Right fielder**—The right fielder must have a strong, accurate throwing arm. This player backs up first base on all bunted balls, on all throws from the catcher to first base, and on all plays when there is a possibility of the ball coming into right field, such as a wild throw. The right fielder also backs up second base on all balls hit to the left side of the diamond.

**Designated hitter**—A designated hitter (DH) can bat for anyone playing defense. The DH often bats in place of the weakest hitter in the lineup. In some leagues, a DH hits instead of the pitcher. The DH is a power slugger, capable of getting the big hit.

## Keeping Score

Using a baseball scorebook is easy once you know the numbering system and a few abbreviations. Each position is assigned a number (see Figure 6.8).

| | |
|---|---|
| **1**—pitcher | **6**—shortstop |
| **2**—catcher | **7**—left fielder |
| **3**—first baseman | **8**—center fielder |
| **4**—second baseman | **9**—right fielder |
| **5**—third baseman | |

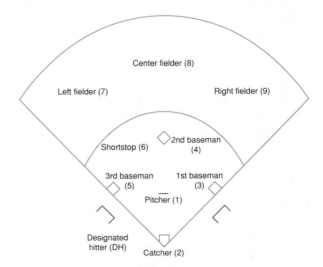

**Figure 6.8** Player positions in baseball.

Every kind of baseball play has a standard abbreviation. Figure 6.9 shows how to use these symbols when keeping a scorebook.

**AB**—Times at bat
**B**—Bunt
**BB**—Walk
**BK**—Balk
**DP**—Double play
**E**—Error
**F**—Foul fly
**FC**—Fielder's choice
**FO**—Fly-out
**G**—Ground ball
(unassisted infield out)
**H**—Hits
**HP**—Hit by pitch
**IW**—Intentional walk
**K**—Strike out
**Kc**—Called third strike
**L**—Line drive
**O**—Out
**OS**—Out stealing
**PB**—Passed ball
**R**—Runs
**RBI**—Runs batted in
**SH**—Sacrifice
**SB**—Stolen base
**TP**—Triple play
**WP**—Wild pitch

Every time a batter goes to the plate, use the numbers to indicate how the player was retired or reached base. For instance, the batter who grounds out to the shortstop is retired 6-3 in your scorebook (see Figure 6.9a). If he or she flies to the right fielder, record FO-9 (see Figure 6.9b). If the batter fouls out to the right fielder, use 9F (see Figure 6.9c). If a batter reaches first base on an error by the second baseman, steals second, goes to third on a wild pitch, and scores on a passed ball, your scorebook would look like Figure 6.10.

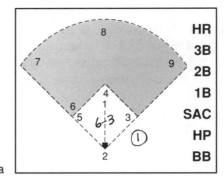

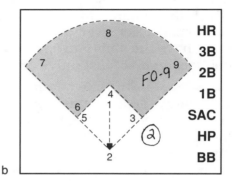

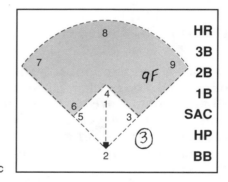

**Figure 6.9** Keeping a scorebook: (a) batter grounds out to the shortstop and is retired, (b) batter flies to the right fielder, and (c) batter fouls out to the right fielder.

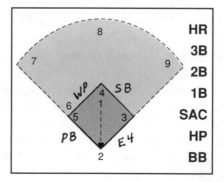

**Figure 6.10** Another scorebook example. Here a batter reaches first base on an error by the second baseman, steals second, goes to third on a wild pitch, and scores on a passed ball.

## UNIT 7

# What Baseball Skills and Drills Should I Teach?

In Unit 4 you learned how to teach baseball skills and how to plan practices. Now it's time to consider exactly what baseball skills to emphasize and what drills to use to help your players develop those skills.

Baseball involves many skills, and you can't teach them all at once. So the best approach is to break them down into offensive and defensive categories. Start with the most basic individual skills and progress your players through more difficult techniques. Defensive skills include throwing, pitching, and catching, which includes catching pitches, throws, and fly balls, and fielding ground balls. Offensive skills include hitting and baserunning.

### Throwing

Throwing is one of the most important skills in baseball. Stress to your players that accuracy is more important than speed—many young players tend to throw very wildly in their attempts to put some zip on the ball.

Teach your players to throw over the top and not sidearm. Throwing the ball over the top will give players greater control and accuracy. Conversely, throwing sidearm can lead to bad throwing habits, wildness, and undue strain on young elbows.

## Overhand Throw

A player's throwing motion is like a set of fingerprints—everyone has one, but it's slightly different from anyone else's. However, to throw a baseball well, every player must use some type of grip, windup, delivery, and follow-through. Here is the overhand throwing technique to teach your players:

### Grip

Grip the ball with the index and middle fingers spaced slightly apart and across the seams of the ball. Place the thumb on the laces, directly under the top fingers. The fingers are on top of the ball when the throwing hand is back.

### Windup

Bring the throwing arm back and up, turning so the front shoulder is pointed at the target. At this point, the weight is on the back foot. The glove hand points toward the target. The arm extends behind the body with wrist cocked and elbow bent (see Figure 7.1a).

### Delivery

Now pick up the lead foot and stride toward the target. As the lead foot touches the ground, turn the hips so that the throwing-side hip drives toward the target (see Figure 7.1b). Transfer the weight from the back foot to the front foot, and bring the throwing arm forward just before releasing the ball (see Figure 7.1c). Encourage young players to look at their target when throwing.

### Follow-Through

Point the throwing hand at the target and swing the back leg around. Bring the throwing arm down in front of the body and end with the feet parallel, in a balanced ready position (see Figure 7.1d).

## Throwing Drills

*Name.* **Target Drill**

*Purpose.* To help players learn the proper release point for throws of various distances and thereby increase their throwing accuracy

*Organization.* Players stand about 10 feet from the backstop with a number of balls. Using towels, create a series of targets at different heights on the backstop. Executing the proper fundamentals, the players practice their release point by trying to hit the targets. Players retrieve their own balls. After several successful throws, players can increase the distance to 15, 20, 25 feet, and so on (Figure 7.2).

*Coaching Points.* You can have four or five stations going at the same time if you use both sides

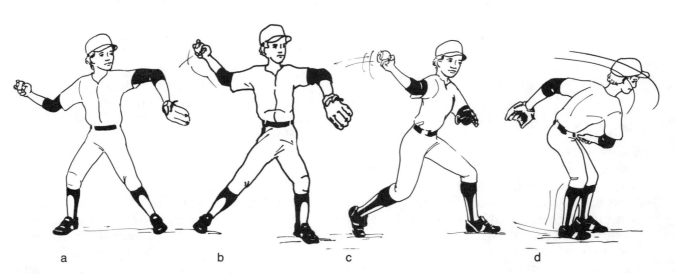

**Figure 7.1** The overhand throw: (a) windup, (b) hips driving toward the target, (c) weight transfer and release, and (d) follow-through.

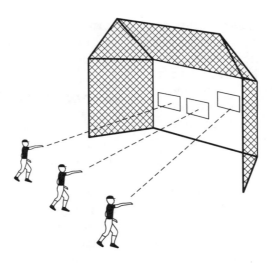

**Figure 7.2**   Target drill.

of the backstop. Watch that your players bring the ball over the top rather than throw sidearm. Players should stride toward the target—doing so leads to a proper follow-through and less strain on the arm.

*Name.*   **Base Relay**

*Purpose.*   To increase the speed and accuracy of throws

*Organization.*   Separate the team into three groups. Position bases at regulation distances in the infield, right field, and left field. Have one group go to each of the three diamonds, with players in each group distributing themselves evenly among the four bases. Start the ball at one base simultaneously for each group. See which group can most quickly relay the ball around the bases while committing the fewest errors. Each player must tag the base while in control of the ball before throwing it on to the next base.

*Coaching Points.*   Very young players cannot grip the ball in their thumb, fingers, and top part of the palm. They will have to use the whole hand. Encourage your bigger players to hold the ball with the thumb and fingers and not in the palm. Emphasize good, quick throws between the bases. As players improve, have them rotate right after they throw the ball.

## Sidearm and Three-Quarter Arm Throws

Although you may teach the proper overhand throwing technique to all your players, count on having to correct them for dropping the arm in the delivery. Many players use the three-quarter arm throw, but it is

---

### Error Detection and Correction for Overhand Throws

In the excitement of the game, players often rush their throws. This is especially true of young players after they field the ball.

| ERROR | CORRECTION |
|---|---|
| Players rush their throws after fielding the ball, which causes them to miss their targets. | 1. Remind the player that he or she must first field the ball properly. |
| | 2. The player then picks the ball from the mitt. |
| | 3. The player sets the feet and uses good mechanics for the grip, windup, delivery, and follow-through. |

often the sign of a tired arm, especially if a pitcher starts using it. A player should use the sidearm throw only when there is no other choice or when throwing from a short distance for a tag out. Improper throwing technique at an early age can lead to bad throwing habits later in a player's career.

The best way to monitor throwing technique is to watch players during warm-up. If you see them using improper mechanics or lapsing into three-quarter arm or sidearm motion, you'll be right there to show them the correct grip, windup, delivery, and follow-through of the overhand throwing technique.

## Pitching

Any baseball coach will tell you that a big percentage of a team's success or failure relates to the quality of its pitchers. Find a successful baseball team, and you'll also find a good pitching staff.

A pitcher needs a strong and accurate throwing arm. Young hurlers should work on controlling their fastballs before trying to master other pitches. A good fastball and, perhaps, an effective change-up are the only pitches a young thrower really needs.

Youngsters who experiment with a curve ball often have trouble getting the ball over the plate. And too many kids injure their arms by throwing breaking pitches incorrectly.

As coach, you should monitor closely the technique, type, and number of pitches your players throw. Your league should have a pitch count or standards for the number of innings a pitcher can pitch in a week, but don't automatically push your pitchers to the limit. Watch them closely, and relieve them if they complain of tightness or soreness in their throwing arm or you notice them tiring.

In working with young pitchers, make clear that good pitching takes good practice. Pitching skills won't develop by just throwing the ball, but pitchers can learn by throwing at a target, facing a hitter in the batter's box, and trying to use a consistent, correct delivery.

Break the pitching motion down into six component skills. By teaching pitchers these components, you will develop a successful pitching staff and prevent injuries to your pitchers' arms.

### Gripping the Ball

Teach your players that holding the ball in their fingertips—as opposed to jamming it into the hand—will help them get good velocity and wrist snap for control. Have your pitchers vary grips on the seams to experiment with the fastball and change-ups. For example, gripping the ball *with* the seams causes the pitch to sink; gripping the ball *across* the seams makes the pitch appear to rise (see Figure 7.3a-b).

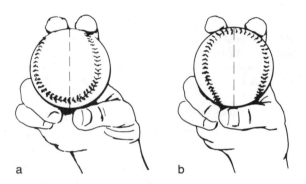

**Figure 7.3**  Gripping the ball: (a) with the seams, and (b) across the seams.

### Delivery

As with general throws from the field of play, the overhand delivery is the most effective throwing motion for young pitchers. The overhand technique ensures maximum control and puts less strain on young arms.

### Windup

The pitching motion begins with the windup. Keeping the front part of the ball-side foot in contact with the plate side of the pitching rubber, the pitcher shifts the weight to the back leg and takes a backward step (see Figure 7.4a).

### Pivot

The pivot is the most essential part of the pitching motion. During the pivot, the pitcher keeps the weight balanced and eyes toward the target. The pitcher pivots on the ball of the front (ball-side) foot to turn it parallel to the rubber. At this point, the pitcher shifts the weight forward onto the pivot foot and lifts the opposite leg into the air (see Figure 7.4b).

## Stride

From the pivot and leg lift, the pitcher must drive the back foot off the rubber and stride toward the plate with the kick leg. The length of the stride depends on the height of the pitcher and what feels most comfortable. Too long a stride makes the ball go high; too short a stride makes the ball go low. Have your pitchers experiment to find out what stride works best.

During the striding motion, the striding or glove-side foot remains closed, as Figure 7.4c shows (the stride foot points toward third base for a right-handed pitcher). The moment before the foot lands, it opens and points toward the plate (see Figure 7.4d).

When the foot opens, the hips open, which brings the upper body through.

The toe and heel of the striding foot should land simultaneously (although the ball of the foot takes most of the shock), land in the same spot with each pitch, and land softly to avoid any jarring in the delivery. The front knee bends so it can absorb the impact of landing with full weight on the front foot. Keeping the knee straight causes undue stress and strain on the front leg.

## Follow-Through

A good follow-through is critical for speed, control, and proper fielding position. As the pitcher releases the ball, the wrist snaps after coming over the top. The arm snaps across the body, and, ideally, the pivot (ball-side) foot swings around to a position that squares the pitcher up to the plate (see Figure 7.4e). The pitcher's eyes must be on the target in preparation to field any balls hit back to the mound.

**Figure 7.4** The pitching motion: (a) weight shift and backward step on the windup, (b) weight shift onto the pivot foot and opposite leg lifted into the air, (c and d) proper stride-leg action, and (e) follow-through.

Advanced pitchers can be concerned with the location of their pitches (for example, outside corner). Young pitchers should simply focus on getting the ball across the plate, in the strike zone.

Here are some key points to emphasize with young pitchers:

- Make sure the catcher is in the crouching position, providing a target (mitt) at all times.
- Use the legs, not the arm, to shift the weight toward the plate.
- Be relaxed and in control throughout the pitching motion.
- Keep your eyes on the target throughout the pitching motion. Don't overthrow!
- Follow through and be ready to field at the end of the motion.
- Make the first pitch a strike every time to get ahead of the hitter.

## Pitching Drills

*Name*. **Seam Drill**

*Purpose*. To emphasize gripping the ball with and across the seams

*Organization*. Teammates pair off and stand 30 to 40 feet apart. Before one line of players throws the balls to their partners, you say, "Grip the ball across the seams" or "Grip the ball with the seams." Throwers check their grips and repeat out loud what you've said before throwing. Repeat the same procedure for the return throws.

*Coaching Points*. Take turns standing behind each line of players to watch ball flight. A correctly thrown across-the-seams ball will rise instead of drop, as a with-the-seams ball does.

*Name*. **Chair Drill**

*Purpose*. To teach young pitchers how to throw over the stride leg, roll the back foot, and finish the pitching motion toward the glove-side hand so they are in a position to field the ball

*Organization*. Set a folding chair 20 to 30 feet from home plate. Have the player place the pivot foot on the chair, instep down (see Figure 7.5a). The stride leg is out in front of the chair, and the foot is aiming at the target. Leaning back for momentum, the pitcher then throws to the target. The pivot foot rolls (heel toward third base for a right-handed pitcher; heel toward first base for a left-handed pitcher) but does not come off the chair (see Figure 7.5b).

*Coaching Points*. Pitchers should concentrate on getting the nose out in front of the toes and following through with the elbow outside the stride-leg knee. Pitchers should not throw hard during this drill. Repetition of the correct stride motion is what's important.

*Name*. **Tarp Target Drill**

*Purpose*. To help pitchers develop better control

*Organization*. Tie a large piece of carpet on an 8-foot by 8-foot section of a backstop. Place a tarp on the target and outline a strike zone in paint or tape (see Figure 7.6). Place a home plate in front of the strike zone. From two-thirds or regulation distance, a hurler throws pitches at the strike zone on the tarp. After throwing 20 balls, they collect the balls and start over. Have the pitchers deliver half of the pitches from the stretch.

---

### Error Detection and Correction for Pitching with Runners on Base

Pitchers often get flustered by runners on base. They should work on pitching from the stretch (see page 70) and focusing on the batter, not the runner.

| ERROR | CORRECTION |
|---|---|
| With a runner on base, the pitcher gets distracted and loses control of the pitches. | 1. Remind the pitcher not to rush the delivery from the stretch. |
| | 2. From the stretch position, the pitcher must still lift the knee and rotate the hips rather than stepping straight to the plate with no lift or rotation. |
| | 3. The pitcher shouldn't shorten the arm motion when throwing from the stretch. |

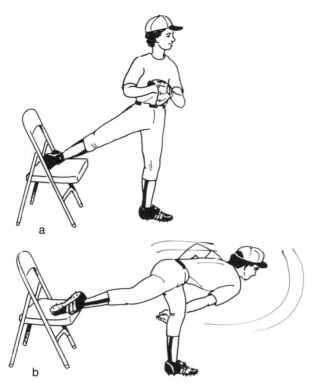

**Figure 7.5** Chair drill: (a) pivot foot on chair, instep down, and (b) pivot foot rolls but does not come off the chair.

*Coaching Points.* As your pitchers' control improves, divide the strike zone into sections (see Figure 7.6) and challenge them to deliver their pitches to the different sections. Pitchers can also work on their pick-off moves into the tarp.

*Name.* **Pitcher's Control Drill**

*Purpose.* To help pitchers develop awareness of the strike zone

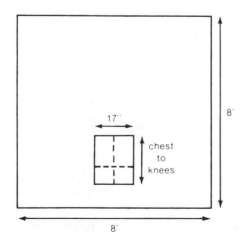

**Figure 7.6** Tarp target drill.

*Organization.* Pitchers and catchers stand at regulation distance from each other. The catcher stands behind home plate, and a batter stands in the batter's box. The batter should alternate between a left- and right-handed batting stance after every five pitches, but not take any swings. The catcher calls balls and strikes. Have the batter wear a helmet in this practice situation.

*Coaching Points.* This gamelike drill will help your pitchers develop a consistent pitching motion, get a good feel for the strike zone, and get use to pitching with a player in the batter's box.

## Catching

A third major defensive skill is catching. This includes catching a thrown ball, catching a grounder hit off a bat, and catching a fly ball.

Initially, some players will be afraid of catching a baseball. That fear will make them flinch right before the ball reaches the glove. They'll end up dropping the ball instead of catching it, or, worse, the ball may hit them. By that time, they may be ready to quit.

Teaching players the correct catching technique is not easy. You must first overcome their fear of getting hit by a hard ball. That's why it's so much better to start kids with safety balls that don't hurt. Players can miss the ball, even get konked on the head with it, and not wind up with a big bump and bruise. When your players have mastered catching the safety ball, you can introduce easy catching with a regulation baseball.

To catch a baseball, the player should position the glove according to the flight of the ball. If the ball is below the waist, the fingers and the palm of the glove hand should be pointed down with the mitt fully open (see Figure 7.7a). If the ball is chest high, the fingers and the palm of the glove should be pointing out, with the thumbs pointing to the sky (see Figure 7.7b). If the ball is above the chest, the fingers point toward the sky (see Figure 7.7c).

In all catching attempts, a player should

1. keep eyes on the ball;
2. have both hands ready, with arms relaxed and extended toward the ball;

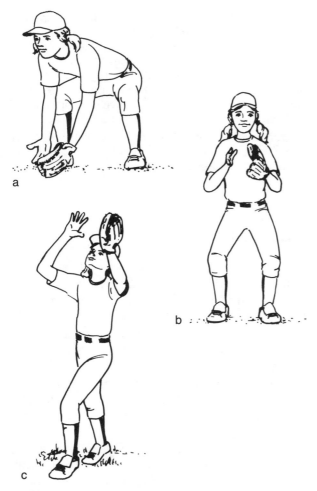

**Figure 7.7** Catching the ball (a) below the waist, (b) chest high, and (c) above the chest.

3. bend the elbows to absorb the force of the throw (see Figure 7.8); and
4. watch the ball into the glove and squeeze it.

**Figure 7.8** Proper position in preparing to catch the ball.

After the catch, the player should immediately grip the ball with the throwing hand in the correct overhand throwing technique.

## Catching Pitchers

The catcher's position is the most demanding in baseball. During the course of a game, the catcher is the busiest player on the field—crouching behind the plate, blocking balls, keeping track of the count on each batter, repositioning teammates defensively, and so on. So select a sturdy, smart, and strong youngster to be your catcher.

A catcher's mitt is padded and rounded so that the ball easily lands in the pocket. The extra padding also helps ensure the safety of the player using the glove.

### Basic Position

The catcher assumes a comfortable crouching position about 2 feet behind the plate. The catcher uses her or his glove to give the pitcher a throwing target (see Figure 7.9). The catcher can move the target around the plate to give the pitcher an inside or outside target. Have catchers protect the throwing hand from foul-tipped balls by placing it behind the back of the leg.

With the legs shoulder-width apart, the catcher keeps the weight on the balls of the feet so he or she is ready to move in any direction for a poorly thrown ball. Staying low helps the catcher avoid being hit by the swing of the batter and allows the umpire to see the baseball as it crosses the plate.

When a ball is pitched in the dirt, the catcher should try to block the ball and keep

**Figure 7.9** Basic catcher's position.

it in front of the body. For example, if a ball is thrown in the dirt to the catcher's right, she or he steps out with the right leg, keeping the ball in the center of the body. The catcher's left leg drags behind while the glove moves between the legs, as shown in Figure 7.10. The catcher makes the same movements on pitches thrown in the dirt to the left side.

When a pitch is thrown in the dirt just in front of the catcher, he or she drops both knees to the ground and slides into the ball. With the back side of the glove on the ground, the catcher places the glove between the legs to execute the block. Bowing the back and bringing the chin down to the chest protects the throat area and helps the catcher keep the eyes on the ball.

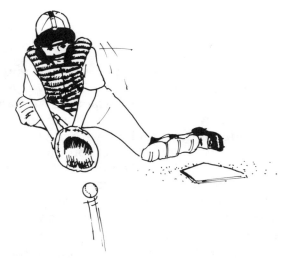

**Figure 7.10** Catcher blocking a ball thrown in the dirt to the right.

### Throwing Out Base Runners

With runners on base, your catcher should be in the *up* position: Feet shoulder-width apart and the right foot slightly in front of the left. The glove hand should be extended away from the body, providing a large target. The back should remain parallel to the ground (see Figure 7.11). This position will allow your catcher to receive the pitch and throw to a base quickly.

When a runner attempts a steal, the catcher should lean into the ball just before catching it, making sure not to come forward too soon, which could lead to an interference call if the batter swings and hits the catcher.

**Figure 7.11** Catcher in the *up* position.

While catching the ball, the catcher should quickly move the glove-side leg forward into the throwing position (jump turn), rotate the shoulders parallel to the batter's box, and bring the glove hand near the ear, where it should meet the throwing hand. The catcher can make the throw by transferring weight from the back leg to the front leg, rotating the shoulders, and following through. The follow-through involves bringing the throwing hand to the opposite knee while stepping toward second base with the throwing-side leg.

## Drills for Catchers

*Name.* **Foul Ball Drill**

*Purpose.* To improve catchers' abilities to react quickly to pop flys

*Organization.* The catcher assumes the crouched position while the partner, standing directly behind the catcher, throws the pop fly. The catcher first turns her or his back to the field, locates the ball, discards the mask, and makes the catch with two hands.

*Coaching Points.* The catcher should not take off the mask until he or she has located the foul ball and is in a position to catch it. A catcher who takes off the mask too early may trip over it.

*Name.* **Shift and Block Drill**

*Purpose.* To teach young catchers how to react properly to wild pitches

*Organization.* Catchers pair up wearing full gear and take turns blocking tennis balls thrown in the dirt near where home plate would be. Players can do this drill quickly. Give them 10 chances per round. Keep track of who controls the most "wild pitches."

*Coaching Points.* Watch that the catcher is getting the body in front of the ball to stop it from going to the backstop.

## Catching Ground Balls

Now that you know how to teach the fundamentals of catching thrown balls, let's look at how you can instruct players to catch balls that have been hit. We'll begin by describing how to teach players to catch balls hit on the ground. These are the five subcomponents of the skill to emphasize: ready position, move to the ball, field, skip and throw, and follow-through.

### Ready Position

To assume the ready position, your players should have their feet slightly wider apart than the shoulders, their knees bent, and their weight over the balls of their feet (see Figure 7.12). The hands hang low between the legs, with the glove open wide. From this ready position, the player can get a good jump on the ball and move quickly in the direction it is hit.

**Figure 7.12**  Ready position for fielding ground balls.

### Move to the Ball

When a ground ball is hit in the direction of an infielder, the player moves to position his or her body in front of the ball. Teach your players to always lead with the glove, no matter which direction they move. This will help them stay low to the ground—the correct position for fielding a ball. Infielders should judge the speed and spin of the ball to determine where they need to move for good fielding position. With practice, players will learn to ''pick a hop,'' or anticipate where the ball will bounce nearest and

highest to them and then move there to catch the ball.

### Field

Here are the steps for teaching your players proper fielding position for ground balls:

1. Bend the knees and keep the glove open.
2. Extend the arms in front of the body and reach out for the ball. The glove-side foot is forward.
3. Watch the ball all the way into the glove and trap it with the throwing hand (see Figure 7.13a).
4. Keep the backside low and field the ball in the middle of the body, cushioning it with ''soft'' hands into the body, to the belt area (see Figure 7.13b).

### Skip and Throw

The skip-and-throw technique will help your infielders get rid of the ball quickly after they've fielded it. While cushioning the ball into the glove, the infielder lines up the glove-side shoulder and hip with the throwing target. With eyes focused on the target and the glove in the center of the chest, the player skips forward and prepares to throw (see Figure 7.13c). As the throwing hand leaves the glove, the arm extends down and back in a comfortable, relaxed position. Pushing off the back leg, the player then throws over the top, moving the throwing shoulder and arm forward quickly (see Figure 7.13d). A strong wrist snap at the point of release will result in better accuracy.

### Follow-Through

During the follow-through, the player points the throwing-side shoulder toward the target and lifts the back leg off the ground. The player's momentum should be forward, in the direction of the throw.

## Drills for Infielders

*Name.* **Hockey**

*Purpose.* To practice fielding fundamentals and game reactions in situations where players can't predict the bounce of the ball

**Figure 7.13** Fielding a ground ball: (a) watch the ball into the glove and trap it with the throwing hand, (b) cushion the ball to the belt area, (c) skip forward and prepare to throw, and (d) push off the back leg and throw the ball over the top.

*Organization.* Separate players into two teams, and put one team on each side of the backstop, which serves as the goal. Each team rotates a "goalie" to defend the goal (about 10 feet wide). The coaches hit ground balls in an attempt to score on the goalies.

*Coaching Points.* Start out slow and increase the tempo as the game goes on. Make sure that the players field the ball out in front of the body and that the head is down on the ball as it enters the mitt.

*Name.* **Pickups**

*Purpose.* To improve players' ability to move and field ground balls

*Organization.* Have the players pair off, each pair having two balls, and stand about 9 feet apart. One player rolls one ball at a time, alternating grounders to the right and left side of the fielder. The fielder fields each grounder and then throws it back to the

partner. After 10 grounders to each side, the roller and the fielder switch roles.

*Coaching Points.* Remind players to slide to the ball—keeping the hips facing forward, not turned—and to field it out in front of the body with the knees bent and the backside low.

*Name.* **Short-Hop Drill**

*Purpose.* To give players practice fielding balls that take short hops

*Organization.* Players pair off and stand in even lines 20 yards apart. The players take turns throwing each other one-hoppers, both long and short ones. The player fielding the ball should make a crisp return throw to the partner.

*Coaching Points.* Make sure that the player keeps the body in front of the ball, keeps the head down (you should be able to see the button on the top of the baseball cap), judges the hop, and watches the ball into the glove.

---

### Error Detection and Correction for Fielding Ground Balls

Players often get a good jump on ground balls hit to their left or right, but when they arrive at the ball their arms are stiff, so the ball hits the glove and bounces out.

| ERROR | CORRECTION |
|---|---|
| Players misfield the ball when they have to field it on the run. | 1. Tell players to concentrate on the ball as they move toward it. |
| | 2. Instruct them to keep the seat and hands low and hands in front of the body. |
| | 3. Remind players to see the ball into the glove. |
| | 4. Emphasize that players cushion the ball to the belt area by pulling the arms in toward the midsection. |

---

## Catching Fly Balls

Sound team defense includes a core of capable outfielders. But developing good skills in the outfield requires diligent practice.

Like their teammates in the infield, outfielders must be in the ready position and prepared for action on each pitch. It's easy for young players to lose concentration in the outfield because they're so far away from most of the action. It's your job to convince your outfielders that they must be alert: knees slightly bent, feet squared and facing home plate, weight on the balls of the feet, and gloves waist-high.

### Judging the Ball

Baseball is a game of quick action and reaction. Defensive players must move to the ball at full speed. Most young athletes tend to drift to the ball, which means they arrive at the point of contact just as the ball does, instead of earlier.

Here's a drill designed to break players of this habit (go-look drill, p. 55): Toss an easy high fly ball a short distance from the player; encourage the player to run full speed to where he or she thinks the ball will come down and to try to catch it in a proper position. Explain that this quick positioning makes the ball easier to catch.

Teach players these tips for catching fly balls properly once they have run to them:

- Maintain eye contact with the ball at all times.
- Whenever possible, position yourself behind the ball.
- Run with the glove down, in a typical sprinting position.
- Communicate by shouting "mine" or "I got it" at least twice.
- Keep hands down until in position to make the catch.
- Catch the ball in front of the head—using two hands if possible—with the arms almost fully extended (see Figure 7.14).

**Figure 7.14**   Basic position for catching a fly ball.

- As the catch is made, give with the impact by bringing the glove down and in toward the chest.
- Always get back as fast as possible on a ball hit over your head. Keep the ball in front of you.

A good throw from the outfield finishes a strong defensive play. After catching the ball with two hands, the player makes a little hop forward to distribute the weight on the back leg. As she or he lines up the hip, shoulder, and glove with the target (second base, third base, or home plate), the arm extends loosely behind. The player's weight comes forward, and the player pushes hard off the throwing-side leg while releasing the ball from an overhand position. The momentum of the throw brings the back leg off the ground, and the player continues to move forward after the throw. Accurate, low, one-bounce throws are best. Unit 8 covers relay throws and cutoffs.

## Drills for Outfielders

*Name.* **Volleyball**

*Purpose.* To emphasize the need to communicate in the outfield

*Organization.* Create two teams, use the foul fence or home run fence as the "net," and form out-of-bounds lines on both sides of the fence. Players throw pop-ups back and forth over the fence. A team scores a point if the ball lands on the ground on the opposite side. Encourage your players to call out for the ball.

*Coaching Points.* Players must communicate on the field to know who is going to catch the ball. Executed properly, this drill can help prevent injuries from collisions in the outfield.

*Name.* **Go-Look Drill**

*Purpose.* To improve players' ability to catch balls on the run

*Organization.* Divide your players into two lines. The lines should be approximately 20 yards apart with the coach between them. Alternating lines, the player behind the first player calls out, "Go." Upon this command, the player in front takes off from the line (see Figure 7.15). The coach throws a pop fly and calls out, "Look." The fielder then locates the ball and breaks to catch it.

*Coaching Points.* With two coaches, you could do both lines simultaneously. Watch that each player concentrates on the ball after locating it. Be sure that you loft the ball high enough so the outfielder has time to get into position and catch it.

*Name.* **Blind Toss**

*Purpose.* To teach players to react to a hit instead of anticipating one

*Organization.* A player stands about 20 feet away from you with her or his back to you. When you yell "ball," toss a ball high into the air. The player turns around, locates the ball, and catches it.

*Coaching Points.* This drill is a confidence builder. It teaches players that they can get to a ball much quicker than they think they can.

## Hitting

Hitting a baseball is one of the most difficult skills to master in this sport. Combine this fact with your players' age and inexperience and you've got your work cut out for you. Good hitters perform the skill in one fluid motion. But to learn how to hit, young players need to be taught four hitting components separately: grip, stance, stride, and swing. Over time, if you emphasize hitting

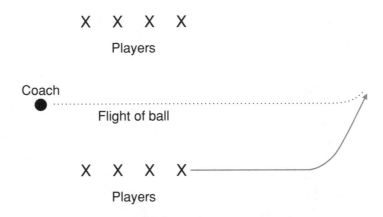

**Figure 7.15** Go-look drill.

fundamentals and offer your players lots of practice and encouragement, even the little tyke who could barely hit one past the pitcher's mound will be grooving hits to the outfield.

## Grip

Teach your players to grip the bat with their fingers, not with the palms of their hands (middle knuckles should be lined up). The bat should be held loosely until the ball actually begins toward the plate; then the grip should be tightened.

## Stance

Players need to be comfortable in the batter's box. The stance that feels good to one player may feel awkward to another. Don't try to make every batter assume the same stance at the plate, but do stress these basics:

- Feet 2 feet wider than the shoulders, set in a square stance
- The back foot parallel to the back line of the batter's box
- The front foot parallel with the front line of the box, toes pointing toward the plate
- Knees bent slightly with weight centered on the balls of the feet, distributed 60% over the back foot and 40% over the front
- Upper body bent slightly at the waist, eyes focused on the pitcher (see Figure 7.16)

**Figure 7.16** Proper batting stance.

- Bat held at a 45° angle to the hands
- Elbows out from the body and flexed, pointing down at the ground
- Feet far enough back from the plate so the bat passes slightly across the outer edge of the plate when the arms are fully extended

## Stride

As the pitcher begins the windup, the hitter must begin to rotate the front shoulder, hip, and knee inward. This is the trigger motion. The slight rotation causes the hands to move 3 to 4 inches backward. The hip rotation and the turning of the knee inward causes the player's weight to shift 60% over the back foot and 40% over the front. A hitter doesn't need to stride to hit. As the saying goes, "Bury the toe and put on a show."

However, if a player does stride, it should be very small. The weight is on the inside part of the back foot after a player completes the stride, and the hands are cocked in a trigger position just off the back shoulder. If a player is going to stride, be sure he or she strides *to* hit, not strides *and* hits at the same time.

---

### Bailing Out on Inside Pitches

Young players have a tendency to step back with the lead foot or fall backward out of the batter's box on inside pitches. A crafty pitcher will exploit this tendency. So teach all your hitters how to open up on inside pitches. And assure them that they'll still have plenty of time to avoid being hit by pitches that are truly coming at them.

---

## Swing

The legs and hips initiate the swing. As the hitter shifts the weight to the front foot, the back foot pivots and the back knee rotates. During this sequence there is a 60% to 40% transfer of weight to the front foot. The front foot remains straight and firm, the shoulders open, and the hands come down and through. The hitter should keep the barrel of the bat above the hands during the swing (see Figure 7.17) to allow hitting down on

**Figure 7.17**  Keeping the barrel of the bat above the hands during the swing.

the ball instead of uppercutting and hitting pop-ups. The lead elbow points toward the ground. The hitter should keep the head still during the swing. The bat should be parallel to the ground as it moves through the hitting zone. Teach your players to hit the ball down and through.

## Hitting Drills

*Name.*  **T-Ball Drill**

*Purpose.*  To help hitters develop a smooth, compact swing

*Organization.*  Set up a batting tee on top of home plate about 6 feet from the backstop. Using the plate allows hitters to orient their stances to the plate and not the tee. Have players work in pairs, one placing balls on the tee while the other hits. Move the tee to different areas on the plate so players can practice hitting different pitches.

*Coaching Points.*  This drill is a great introduction to hitting for any young player. It develops all the skills required to make good contact on the ball. Stress to the players that they concentrate on contact and watch the ball as they swing. Batting tees are easy to make out of radiator hose, pipes, and a wooden base.

*Name.*  **Soft-Toss Drill**

*Purpose.*  To improve weight transfer, body control, and timing

*Organization.*  This drill uses at least two players, a net or fence to hit into, and a dozen or more balls to hit. Set up the hitter with a partner kneeling about 10 feet away, just off the hitter's front knee (see Figure 7.18). The feeder triggers the hitter's swing by dropping her or his hand just before tossing the ball. The feeder should float the ball to the inside, outside, and middle part of the plate. The hitter must drive the ball into the net or fence.

*Coaching Points.*  Use this drill to help players lose their fear of getting hit by pitches. Have the feeder switch to safety balls and throw harder. Watch each batter's front foot and head. Work with players who bail out or move their head back. Give them plenty of praise for good technique, especially on inside pitches.

*Name.*  **Tire Drill**

*Purpose.*  To help hitters develop strong wrists, hands, and forearms

---

### *Error Detection and Correction for Hitting*

Given the complexity of hitting, hitters can make numerous mistakes. The list here includes some common errors and ways to correct them:

| ERROR | CORRECTION |
|---|---|
| Overstriding and lunging | Have player widen stance and reduce or eliminate the stride |
| No pivot on back foot | Tell hitter to raise the heel of the back foot off the ground and turn the foot in a little |
| Pulling the head and front shoulder | Have pitcher throw to a catcher while the hitter in the box follows the path of the ball to the catcher's mitt |
| Swinging late | Instruct hitter to begin trigger motion sooner |

**Figure 7.18**   Soft-toss drill.

*Organization.*  Take a normal car tire, cut a hole through the middle of the tread, set the tire on a steel fence pole, and place a pin through the pole, under the tire, to allow the tire to spin. Set up the hitter alongside the tire as if in the batter's box next to the plate. Have the hitter cock the wrists, pivot on the back foot, and drive the bat into the tire, forcing it to spin (see Figure 7.19).

*Coaching Points.*  This is a good drill to help players develop the feel of driving through the ball. Have the batter simulate swings on an inside pitch, a pitch down the middle, and a pitch on the outside.

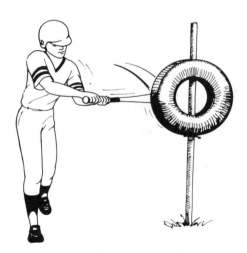

**Figure 7.19**   Tire drill.

## Bunting

Every baseball team needs a variety of offensive weapons—one of these weapons is the bunt. So teach every player on your team how to bunt, and provide lots of practice time so each player feels confident at the skill. The main purpose of the bunt is to advance base runners, but it's also a good surprise strategy to get on base. The bunt is a good tactic for your players to use against overpowering pitchers and against pitchers who end up in poor fielding position on the follow-through.

With runners on first or second base, a successful sacrifice bunt will advance the runners into scoring position. As the pitcher starts the windup, the batter squares around, either by moving the back foot up parallel with the front foot or by pivoting on the heel of the front foot and the toe of the back foot.

The bat is held level or at a 45° angle (the 45° technique is harder to master). The knees bend and the weight is forward to prevent lunging. The upper hand slides 12 inches up the bat and the bottom hand stays on the handle. Players should grip the bat lightly with the upper hand, keeping the fingers underneath and the thumb on top in the form of a *V*. Figure 7.20 shows the basic bunting stance and hand positions.

From the start of the pitcher's delivery to the actual contact of ball and bat, the player must focus on the ball. The hitter's arms are extended to position the bat at the top of the strike zone, covering the entire plate. Letting the ball come to the bat, the batter gives with the arms and hands as the ball is met,

**Figure 7.20**   Basic bunting stance and hand positions.

''catching'' the ball as if the end of the bat were a glove.

Keeping the bat above the ball will prevent making a pop-up, which is the worst thing a batter can do when sacrifice bunting. The batter should also avoid bunting back to the pitcher or hitting the ball hard because the defense could turn a double play. Ideally, the player places the sacrifice bunt right down the third baseline. For a right-handed batter to do this, the player must bring the handle close to the body with the bottom hand. To bunt down the first baseline, the player must push out the handle with the bottom hand.

---

## Bunting Dos and Dont's

Execution is the key to a successful bunt. Here are the most important points you must teach your players to Do and Don't when bunting:

### DO . . .

- keep your eyes on the ball.
- get on top of the ball.
- square the feet around and have the bat at the top of the strike zone.
- bunt only good balls (strikes).
- bend the knees slightly, keeping the weight on the balls of the feet.
- let the hands give as the ball hits the bat.
- move up in the batter's box

### DON'T . . .

- get under the ball.
- commit yourself too soon and lunge or chop at the ball.
- angle the bat on a pitched ball.
- grab the bat with the whole hand; instead use a *V* to hold the thickest part of the bat.
- stand straight up and move the body up or down on the pitched ball.
- adjust to high and low pitches by moving the bat up or down.

---

## Bunting Drills

*Name.* **Reaction Drill**

*Purpose.* To help players learn to move quickly from a hitting to a bunting position

*Organization.* Spread a number of bunters 4 feet apart in a semicircle around you. Players start in a hitting position; then on command they drop down to a bunting position.

*Coaching Points.* Emphasize quickness, and stop each time to check the fundamentals. Later, go through a pitching motion so that players can get used to reacting to the delivery.

*Name.* **Four-Base Target Bunt**

*Purpose.* To give players many opportunities to bunt the ball to a particular area

*Organization.* Split the team into four groups. Each group goes to a base on the infield, which serves as home plate for the drill. Mark a series of semicircles on the infield to the left and right of each base. A designated pitcher for each group throws three balls to each batter, who alternates bunting them to the specified locations. After a turn at one base, the bunter advances to the next base and gets three more balls. The drill is over when players are back at the base where they started.

*Coaching Points.* This fun drill gives everyone plenty of chances to work on bunting. Make sure that your players aren't so eager to move on to the next base that they don't concentrate on hitting the target.

## Baserunning

Helping your players improve their hitting and bunting fundamentals will certainly make their experience more rewarding. But a third skill—baserunning—is just as vital to a successful offense. Unfortunately, many youth teams get runners on base, then make inning-ending baserunning blunders.

---

## Off and Running

Before you can teach players how to run the bases, they first must know how to run. Teach them proper sprinting form—head up, body leaning forward, on the toes, high knee lift, and arms pumping front to back (not across the body).

Don't waste scoring opportunities. Stress baserunning at every practice. Base runners must always know where the ball is, know how many outs there are, pick up signals given by coaches, and know what they will do when the ball is hit. Use the baserunning and sliding instructional tips in the rest of this unit to teach your players to be heads-up, aggressive base runners.

## Running to First Base

When a hitter makes contact, he or she should drop the bat at the end of the swing, then move out of the batter's box as quickly and efficiently as possible. The player turns in the direction of first base, stays low, drives out of the box, and starts down the line with a jab step of the back foot.

The run to first base should be an all-out sprint, and the player should run "through" the bag, like a sprinter hitting the finish-line tape (see Figure 7.21). Tell your players not to lunge or jump at the bag because that is not as fast as a running step. The only time they should slide into first is when a throw pulls the first baseman off the bag, and they can avoid the tag by sliding. Make sure your players are ready to advance to second if the throw to first is a bad one.

If the player hits a ball through the infield or into the outfield, she or he should "think second": Run a flat arc to first base and run hard past the bag, looking for an opportunity to advance to second. The runner begins the flat arc about 6 feet out of the batter's box (no more than 3 or 4 feet out-

side the line) and hits the left inside corner of the base with the left foot. On extra base hits, your base runner should continue the pattern of flat arcs to each base (see Figure 7.22).

If a base runner takes the turn at first, instruct him or her to sprint about a third of the distance to second base. The player will know by the first base coach's commands whether to go to second or return to first.

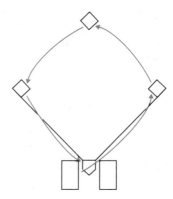

**Figure 7.22**   Running around the bases in a flat arc.

## Baserunning Drill

_Name._  **Running the Bases**

_Purpose._  To give players practice running bases

_Organization._  Each player starts in the batter's box, simulates a swing, and then runs to first base. You stand at first base and call out, "Run through the bag" or "Take a turn" or "Second," loudly enough that the runner can hear your command two or three strides before the bag. Position a coach at second base to direct runners coming from first: "Stay," "Round it," or "Third." The third base coach can give similar instructions to runners reaching third base.

_Coaching Points._  The key to making aggressive turns on the base paths and heading on a straight line from first to second, second to third, or third to home is dipping the left shoulder and leaning the upper body toward the inside of the infield as the player rounds each bag.

## Taking Leadoffs

Once on base, a runner needs to know a leadoff technique. Most effective is the controlled lead because it puts the runner a maximum distance from the base but in a

**Figure 7.21**   Base runner leaning into first base.

good position to get back to the base should the catcher attempt a pickoff.

To start, the runner should assume a relaxed stance with feet no more than shoulder-width apart and weight distributed equally on the feet. To initiate movement, the runner takes a short step with the right foot in direct line to the next base. Keeping the shoulders square to the infield, the player then uses a cross-over step with the left leg and arm motion to get a maximum, yet safe, distance from the bag. When she or he stops, the runner should come down with the knees slightly bent and in a balanced position and the weight in the center of the body (see Figure 7.23).

As soon as the pitcher's body motion indicates the start of the pitch, the runner takes a quick cross-over step to initiate the attempted steal. Getting that split-second jump on the pitcher is often the difference between being out or safe at second base.

**Figure 7.23** A base runner stops with knees slightly bent and weight centered.

## Sliding

When approaching a base, a player must decide in an instant whether to slide. If the play at the base appears close or if a coach or teammate is yelling to get down, the player should slide. And once the decision is made, it should be carried out. Players often change their mind at the last second, which increases the chance of injury. But most injuries result from poor sliding technique. Teach your players how to slide safely and

correctly, and give them plenty of opportunities to practice so that they become comfortable with the actual motion.

Here is the sequence of the bent-leg slide you'll want to teach players:

1. Start the slide 10 to 12 feet from the bag.
2. Don't drop down to the ground—slide to the bag.
3. As you approach the bag, bend your knees (which will drop your hips). Then extend the right leg toward the bag and bend the left leg under the right knee to form a 4.
4. Slide on the buttocks, not on the side or the hips.
5. Tuck chin to chest to prevent banging your head.
6. Your extended foot should be 6 to 8 inches off the ground to slide over the bag.
7. Keep hands up; don't drag them across the ground as you slide.

### Sliding Drill

*Name.* **Slip-and-Slide**

*Purpose.* To teach sliding skills in an easy, nonthreatening exercise

*Organization.* One at a time, the players run hard to the slip-and-slide area (a long plastic sheet) or wet grassy area and attempt to slide. Encourage them to throw out their legs and fly through the air, as shown in Figure 7.24.

*Coaching Points.* Make sure players start their slides just as they reach the plastic. If they run on the slip-and-slide, they can fall and get hurt.

**Figure 7.24** Slip-and-slide drill.

## Tagging Up

When a ball is hit in the air, the runner must decide whether to go halfway to the next base or to tag up. The first or third base coach can help make the call. There's no decision to make on foul fly balls—the runner should always tag up. Outfield flies are tougher, requiring a quick assessment of how deep the ball was hit, the positioning of the outfield, and the throwing arm of the outfielder who is likely to make the catch. Tell your runners that in most situations, they should play it safe and not try to advance, unless you are instructing them from the coach's box to do so. If a runner is going to tag up, she or he needs to stay low, keep the knees bent, and push hard off the bag on the coach's command to "go." The player should be ready to slide into the next base if necessary.

## Young Players' Skill Development

More important than all of the advice we've shared with you in this unit is this: Be patient with your players as they try to learn the many skills required to play baseball. Teach them well the first time, but be prepared to repeat your instructions many times, to the team and to individuals.

You are in a position to help your players appreciate baseball and the techniques involved in playing it successfully. Make the most of your opportunity.

# UNIT
# 8

# *How Do I Get My Players to Play as a Team?*

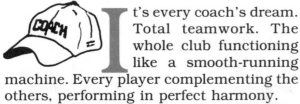

It's every coach's dream. Total teamwork. The whole club functioning like a smooth-running machine. Every player complementing the others, performing in perfect harmony.

But you're a baseball or T-ball coach. And you're realistic. You've got nine young players who look lost as they spread across that big diamond on defense. On offense,

your hitters seem to think that a sacrifice means to force out the base runner nearest to home plate. Teamwork can be a BIG problem.

When you think of baseball tactics, you probably think of the complex plays used by major league teams. And you realize that your players won't execute anything as complicated as, say, a hit and run. But don't let that stop you from teaching your players the team tactics they should know and can learn to execute.

In this unit, you learn how to coordinate all the members of your team so they can participate in games successfully. We explain how to help players take the skills described in Unit 7 and use them within the team framework. Here are the keys to making your ball club a real TEAM:

**T**—Teach players the tactics of the game.

**E**—Emphasize group accomplishments over single players' successes.

**A**—Assign players to positions that they feel comfortable in and that will most benefit individual and team development.

**M**—Make everyone feel part of the team through participation, instruction, and attention.

## Offensive Tactics

The offensive plays you teach should never exceed your players' ability to perform every component skill. For example, don't instruct players in the use of a steal play unless you have taught them how to lead off the base, get a jump on the pitcher, and slide.

Given that your players understand and can perform the skills explained in Unit 7, you can teach them a variety of basic strategies. In addition, you should develop your players' sense of when to use them. Here is a short list of the offensive tactics you might teach your team:

*Steal*—see the explanation on page 61. Additional considerations include watching the delivery of the pitcher, getting a jump on the pitch, and reacting to avoid the tag.

*Delayed steal*—similar to a straight steal, except the runner waits until the catcher's attention is diverted or relaxed. For instance, a runner may wait until a catcher begins to lazily lob the ball back to the pitcher before taking off. By the time the pitcher can catch the throw, the runner can be safely sliding into the base. Another instance of the delayed steal is when the middle infielders do not cover second base after the pitch.

*Double steal*—like a straight steal, except two runners are involved. One version of the double steal calls for the second runner to break for the next base and draw a throw. The lead runner then breaks quickly for the next base.

*Sacrifice bunt*—like a regular bunt, except the batter's sole responsibility is to lay down a bunt so a base runner can advance successfully. The batter will most likely be thrown out at first, but the lead runner will be one base closer to home.

*Sacrifice fly*—when a batter hits a fly ball that scores a runner from third. Young hitters may be unable to do this intentionally, and you should discourage hitters from it if you think it may cause them to drop their back shoulder habitually.

*Hit to opposite field*—generally used in two instances: when a coach wants the hitter to advance a runner on base and when a hitter is having problems keeping focused on the ball or has a slow swing. By concentrating on hitting to the opposite field, the hitter will see the ball longer.

*Take on 3-0 count*—a good strategy against a pitcher who is struggling to get the ball across the plate. The hitter takes the pitch in hopes of a free pass to first base.

*Run on any ball hit with a 3-2 count and 2 outs*—the runners must move anyway, and this increases the likelihood that they will make it to another base before there is a play. Once the pitcher commits to throwing home, the runners should be off and running.

## Signals to Players

Develop a simple system of hand signals to set any of these plays in motion. Don't overload your players. If they have trouble grasping a tactic or remembering a signal, simplify or drop it. Players can't execute what they can't understand.

## Signaling the Play

Common hand signals to batters and runners can be made easier if the signals to the batter come from one hand and the signals to base runners from the other. Here is a sample of some hitting and baserunning signals you might use (see Figures 8.1a-c).

| *Sign* | *Message to player* |
| --- | --- |
| **Batter** | |
| Right hand across chest | Swing away |
| Right hand to nose | Take pitch |
| Right hand to belt | Bunt |
| Right hand to ear | Sacrifice bunt |
| Rubbing hands together | Wipe-off sign |
| **Base runners** | |
| Left hand to face | Steal |
| Left hand to bill of cap | Delayed steal |
| Left hand pointing | Double steal |
| Left hand patting top of cap | Stay, unless a wild pitch, passed ball, or hit |
| Left hand across chest | Go on contact |

In addition, instruct your players to react to situations that allow them to take advantage of the defense, even when you haven't called a specific play. For example, if a catcher loses control of a pitch, your base runners should be ready to take the next base without your telling them to do so.

You may also need to shout instructions to base runners when a defensive player loses the flight of the ball. Think ahead on each pitch, keeping in mind

- the speed of your base runners,
- the strength of the infielders' and outfielders' arms,
- playing conditions, and
- the score.

### Hitting Strategies

The batter, more than any other offensive player, dictates the offensive strategy. If you have a good contact hitter at the plate who has limited power, you will more likely tell base runners to run with the pitch than with a power hitter up who strikes out a lot. Why?

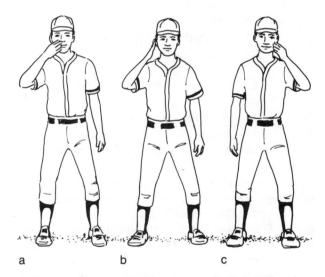

**Figure 8.1** Common hand signals: (a) right hand to nose—take pitch, (b) right hand to ear—sacrifice bunt, and (c) left hand to face—steal.

The contact hitter will probably get the bat on the ball, preventing an easy putout by the catcher on the lead base runner. Second, the batted ball will rarely make it out of the infield, making it easier to get a force-out if the lead runner is not moving on the pitch. But with a power hitter up, you don't want to take the big chance that she or he will miss the pitch (for a strike) and leave the base runner an easy target for the catcher. And because the power hitter is likely to get the ball beyond the infield if contact is made, there is not a big advantage to sending the runner because a force-out is unlikely.

A good hitter should observe the pitcher during warm-ups and on pitches to teammates who bat earlier in the lineup. The hitter can also ask teammates for information about the speed, location, and type of pitches thrown.

Once in the batter's box, the hitter must always be aware of the count, the number of outs, and the coach's signal. A missed sign can result in an easy double play. A received sign that is then executed can be the start of a big inning. So go over all of these signals regularly during your practices. And make the corrections when a sign is missed, so that doesn't happen in a game.

A good hitter is a confident hitter. You can boost any player's hitting confidence by staying positive. If you're praying for a hitter to walk because you doubt he or she can get the bat on the ball, then what do you suppose the team is thinking? So be positive, even when your lineup is retired 1-2-3.

## Offensive Team Drills

_Name_. **Hit and Run**

_Purpose._ To teach hitters to execute proper batting skills and base runners to react to various situations

_Organization._ A coach pitches to a batter at home plate with a runner at first. The coach calls certain plays, such as the hit and run, and then throws the pitch. The hitter must react and hit the ball; the base runner takes a lead and then reacts to the hit.

_Coaching Points._ It's one thing to talk about skills; it's another to perform them under some pressure. This is a good opportunity to evaluate players' skills and performance in a game situation.

_Name_. **Signal and Deliver**

_Purpose._ To teach players to read the coach's signals in a simulated game

_Organization._ Place a defense on the field, but have a coach act as the pitcher. From the third base box, have another coach give signals to hitters and base runners. Players react to the signals and execute the plays.

_Coaching Points._ This is an excellent way for players to develop confidence in reading signals. It also lets you see how players react in game situations.

## Baserunning Strategies

In Unit 7, you learned how to teach players to lead off, turn and run, and steal. But understanding the skills doesn't mean that your players will be effective base runners. They must also know how, when, and why to remain at a base or to run on. Here are a few simple rules of baserunning strategy:

_Watch the pitcher_:
Instruct your players to watch the hurler prepare to pitch the ball. Once the pitcher strides toward home plate, she or he cannot throw to a base, so your base runner can increase the leadoff or try to steal. However, if the pitcher steps toward first base or moves his or her back foot off the rubber, your runner should quickly return to the bag.

_Listen and watch the base coach_:
Explain that the base coach's job is to watch what's going on in the field and to help players run the bases safely. Runners on first base should listen to instructions from the first base coach; runners on second and third base should follow the instructions of the third base coach.

_Do not run unless you are forced to_:
Base runners are not always forced to run. For example, if a runner is on first base and a fly ball is caught in the outfield, the runner is no longer forced to go to second base. She or he can stay at first base. The base coach will tell the base runners when a force is in effect.

_Stay close to the base and tag up on fly balls_:
Make sure your players understand that a caught fly ball is an automatic out. At the youth level, you can send runners halfway to the next base, because about as many fly balls will be dropped as caught. However, if a fly ball is caught, a runner who has left a base must tag up before advancing.

A great reference for you to better understand baserunning and how to teach it is

*High-Percentage Baserunning* (see the last page of this *Guide*).

## Defensive Tactics

A baseball field is too vast for nine young players to cover. And that's even more true when the kids are small and inexperienced and they're not sure where to stand. Effective team defense starts with teaching players correct positioning.

## Positioning

Positioning is a primary concern of any team defense. In baseball, it's not as simple as telling your players that "if your opponent does this, you do this." Instead, you'll have to base your positioning instructions on the

- pitcher's throwing arm,
- pitch's expected speed and location,
- hitter's preferred batting side, and
- hitter's tendencies.

For example, say there's a right-handed pitcher of moderate speed on the mound.

This pitcher often throws to the inside of the plate against left-handed hitters. The left-handed batter at the plate is a pull hitter (typically hitting the ball to the right side of second base). Given all this information, you'd want your fielders to shade toward the right side of the diamond (see Figure 8.2).

But shifting to the right or left is not all there is to consider about defensive positioning. You'll also want players to move up or back, depending on the hitter's estimated power potential. Additional elements of good team defense include backing up each other on the field and efficiently relaying and cutting off throws from the outfield.

## Defensive Backups

In most games and practices, a few throws inevitably get by the fielders. That's why every fielder has backup responsibilities.

In most games involving young or inexperienced players, it isn't so much the initial mistake that hurts but the series of mistakes that follow. In other words, a bad throw to third isn't critical unless no one is there to back up the play and the ball rolls all the way to the fence. An easy out at third turns into a run.

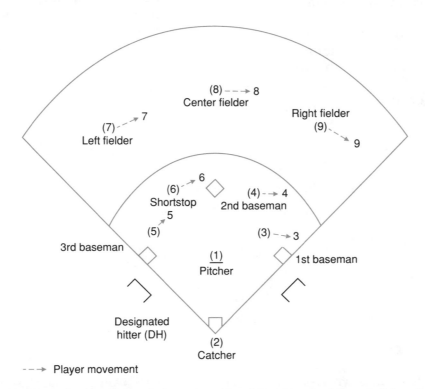

**Figure 8.2**  Fielders shading toward the right side of the diamond for a left-handed pull hitter.

## Relays and Cutoffs

Relays and cutoffs are very important in team defense. Typically, the shortstop and second baseman are responsible for moving out to receive throws from the outfielders and relaying them to the appropriate base. The shortstop handles all relay throws from the left and center fielders, while the second baseman takes throws from the right fielder.

When a fly is hit deep to an outfielder, the appropriate infielder runs toward the outfielder and lines up with the base to which the infielder intends to relay the throw. The weaker the outfielder's arm, the closer the infielder needs to get to the outfielder.

A cutoff player gets in a position between the fielder throwing the ball and the base where the play is to be made. For example, if a runner will definitely score before a throw reaches the plate, the ball should be cut off before it reaches the catcher (see Figure 8.3). The player cutting off the throw either relays the throw to home or throws to another base to make a play on a trailing runner.

Cutoff players should position themselves 15 to 25 feet ahead of the base where the play is to be made. Most throws that are cut off are to third base or home plate. The third baseman is the cutoff on throws from left field, and the first baseman takes all throws from center field over to right field. The shortstop is the cutoff for throws to third base, and the pitcher backs up these throws either at third or at home.

## Specific Defensive Plays

As we've shown, positioning is important, but it's not enough—before a pitch, players should know where to throw if the ball is hit to them.

Consider introducing the following defensive tactics to your team:

*Get the lead runner*—The lead runner is the one farthest advanced on the bases. The defense's objective is to stop the player closest to scoring by throwing the ball to the base that the lead runner is going to.

*Hit the cutoff player*—When a ball is hit deep into the outfield, the outfielder throws the ball to an infielder to shorten the throw, and improve the accuracy. Hitting the cutoff increases the chance of putting out a runner trying to advance to another base.

*Double play*—Turning a double play involves putting out two players in the same play series. This can be done by getting two runners out at different bases. Examples include throwing from second to first, tagging a runner and throwing to a base, and catching a fly ball and throwing it to any base occupied by a runner. A double play can stop a rally and boost the morale of the defensive team. The double play is the pitcher's best friend.

*Back up the throw*—Every player not directly involved in a play should back up

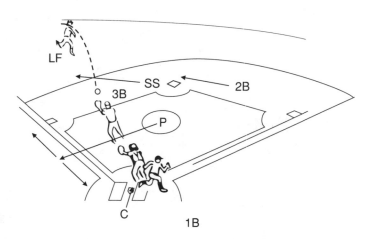

**Figure 8.3**  If a runner will score before a throw reaches the plate, the ball should be cut off.

throws to different parts of the field. The pitcher backs up the base that the lead runner is moving toward, especially if it's home plate. Infielders back up each other when a throw is coming from the catcher.

*Back up the hit*—Outfielders not directly involved in a play back up each other. If the ball gets away from one outfielder, the backup can make the play and prevent runners from taking an extra base.

*Pickoff*—When trying to pick off a base runner, the pitcher works closely with teammates. Usually, the catcher gives the sign to throw to a base. The infielder who will receive the throw may also give the pitcher visual cues, such as putting up the glove or pointing at the bag.

*Give up a run*—Sometimes you'll decide to give up a run in exchange for an out because you have a comfortable lead.

*Get the first out*—In a double play situation, it is critical that the first out be the lead runner. If infielders retire the lead runner, they can attempt to complete the double play.

Again, keep your defensive strategies simple and the number manageable. Stay within your players' stage of development.

Defense in baseball requires quick reactions. If you overload players with too much information or it's too difficult, they won't be able to respond quickly and properly when the ball is hit.

## Defensive Team Drills

*Name*. **Cutoff and Relay Drill**

*Purpose*. To work on the mechanics of relay and cutoff skills and show players how they can contribute to a team defense

*Organization*. Place a team on the field. Each infielder has a ball (except the pitcher and catcher). You stand in shallow outfield and call out the number of runners on base. Each infielder, one at a time, calls out the number of outs and throws a simulated hit to the outfield, anything from a single or a double to a sure out. The drill starts with the third baseman, and the other infielders wait until the previous cutoff or relay play is complete before taking a turn. The catcher directs the cutoff players to their positions and calls the play.

*Coaching Points*. Use every baserunning situation possible to practice the spectrum of cutoff and relay plays. Watch each infielder's and outfielder's throwing, catching, and fielding mechanics, and check that each player makes the proper choice as to where to throw the ball.

*Name*. **Team Throwing for Points Drill**

*Purpose*. To develop throwing accuracy

*Organization*. Assign a player to each position on the field. Teach your players their position numbers as indicated in an official scorebook (pitcher, 1; catcher, 2; first baseman, 3; second baseman, 4; third baseman, 5; shortstop, 6; left fielder, 7; center fielder, 8; right fielder, 9). The pitcher starts the drill by executing a skip and throw to the player whose number you call out. The player fielding the ball then throws it to the player at the position you call out. The team earns points with throws to specific spots on the other players' bodies: the chest earns 5 points, the head 3 points, and the arms and legs 1 point. Throws away from the body subtract points from the team score.

*Coaching Points*. The team's objective is to earn 50 points in as few throws as possible. Each time the team practices this drill, they should try to establish a new "team record" for throws required to reach 50 points.

## Pitching Strategies

The pitcher is the most important defensive player. Quite simply, fielders don't have to field what is not hit to them. If you are fortunate enough to have two or three good pitchers, you're well on your way to having a good defense.

You've probably heard the distinction described between a pitcher and a thrower. A pitcher is a surgeon, exposing each hitter's weakness. (Every hitter has at least one.) The pitcher rarely throws the ball far from the strike zone and thus seldom walks a batter.

In comparison, a thrower simply rears back and fires the ball at the catcher's mitt, figuring the velocity of the pitch will prevent the hitter from making contact. Throwers walk a lot of hitters because of their wildness.

Teach your pitchers to pitch, not just throw. Help them to understand why they shouldn't lob the ball right over the plate when the count is 3-1. In addition to a pitching mind-set, help pitchers develop their mechanics as early as possible; they'll have more success and fewer arm problems.

Another aspect of pitching you'll need to teach is facing hitters when runners are on base. In this situation, the pitcher should begin from the stretch, with the ball-side foot parallel to and touching the rubber (not on top of it). The pitcher's body faces away from home plate and toward either third or first, depending on what side she or he throws from. The stretch position makes it easier for the pitcher to throw to a base to pick off a potential base stealer (see Figure 8.4).

An excellent book on this subject is *Coaching Pitchers*, which you can order through Human Kinetics Publishers (see the last page of this *Guide* for additional information).

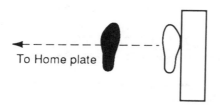
To Home plate

**Figure 8.4**   In the stretch position, the pitcher's ball-side foot is parallel to and touching the rubber.

### Pitching Strategy Drills

*Name.*  **Pitching Out of Trouble**

*Purpose.*  To give pitchers practice at pitching out of a jam

*Organization.*  Put a defensive team out in the field and a runner on each base. You call certain situations, such as hit and run or squeeze bunt. The pitcher must concentrate on retiring each batter.

*Coaching Points.*  Having to pitch out of trouble is one of the most difficult situations facing pitchers. Teach them to keep the ball low and out of the hitter's sight to get the batter to hit a ground ball. Changing speeds will keep the batter off balance. Trying a few pickoffs at first base will also make the batter wait longer for the next pitch, which might disturb his or her concentration.

*Name.*  **Pickoff Move Drill**

*Purpose.*  To practice throwing out runners on the bases

*Organization.*  Put a defensive team out in the field and a runner on each base. From the stretch position, the pitcher practices throwing to first, sec-

ond, and third base. Most pickoff throws will be to first base, so encourage the pitcher to make more throws there than to than second or third. Base runners should practice leading off and returning to the bag. Fielders can practice moving to the bases, catching the ball, and making the tag.

*Coaching Points.*  Watch pitchers closely for balks. If they are throwing to a base and a foot is on the rubber, they must not make a pitching motion toward home. Have runners try to distract pitchers by faking a steal, as opponents will do.

## T-Ball Tactics

Most of the baseball skills and strategies we've covered also apply to T-ball. But there are some differences, which T-ball coaches must know to properly instruct players.

The biggest difference between baseball and T-ball is that in T-ball, batters hit a ball from a tee (see Figure 8.5). T-ball fields are also smaller. The idea of T-ball is to get every player involved in the game. This may mean that 12 or 13 players are on the field at once.

There is not a lot of strategy to T-ball, but you should help your players master the fundamentals of hitting, fielding, throwing, and baserunning. Keep things simple. If your skill instruction is too complicated, you may discourage kids before they even get into the game. As a coach, remember that your players must know how to crawl before they can walk.

**Figure 8.5**   In T-ball, batters hit from a tee.

## Emphasize the Team

Although you'll probably have a few players who are more talented than the rest, stress the importance of teamwork in every activity. A base runner who breaks up a double play should be praised as much as a batter who hits a home run.

The better you are at getting players to appreciate the need to perform together, the more successful your team will be. And, you and your players will enjoy the game more.

## Assign Players to Proper Positions

Players typically show up to the first practice with certain positions in mind. Perhaps one player's favorite major leaguer is a shortstop. Another player's parent may have been a catcher and has primed the child to catch. Still another player may want to be as far from the action as possible and is looking for an outfield position.

Whatever the case, you won't be starting with a clean slate. So the best thing to do is let your players try the positions they request, along with several others that they may be more suited for. Giving young players experience at a variety of positions will help them better determine what position they enjoy most and will help you determine what position they play best.

By mastering both defensive and offensive skills and strategies, your players will enjoy the great game of baseball even more. If your efforts can produce players working to improve both phases of the game and promoting a team effort, winning will take care of itself.

## Let Everyone Participate

It's been said that the quality of a team is best measured by the least-skilled player. That may or may not be true, but a strong bench is common to most successful and happy baseball teams.

As we said in Unit 2, participation is at least as important as success to young players. So even if it means losing a game or two, give all your players roughly equivalent times at bat and opportunities in the field. Letting everyone play and not stressing winning at all costs gives all your players the opportunity to blossom and test their abilities in baseball.

## Sample Season Plan for Beginning Baseball Players

*Goal:* To help players learn and practice the individual skills and team tactics needed to play baseball games successfully.

*T* = Initial teaching time (min)

*P* = Practice and review time (min)

* = Skills practiced during drills and activities

| Skills | Week 1 Day 1 | Day 2 | Week 2 Day 1 | Day 2 | Week 3 Day 1 | Day 2 | Week 4 Day 1 | Day 2 |
|---|---|---|---|---|---|---|---|---|
| Warm-up | T(10) | (10) | (10) | (10) | (10) | (10) | (10) | (10) |
| Cool-down | T(10) | (5) | (5) | (5) | (5) | (5) | (5) | (5) |
| Evaluation | (5) | (5) | (5) | (5) | (5) | (5) | (5) | (5) |
| **Rules** | T(5) | T(5) | T(5) | T(5) | * | * | * | * |
| Signals | | | | | | | | |
| **Throwing** | T(10) | * | * | * | * | * | * | * |
| Drills | P(15) | P(10) | P(10) | | | | | |
| **Catching** | | | | | | | | |
| Throws | T(10) | P(10) | P(10) | P(10) | * | * | * | * |
| Pitches | | | | T(10) | T(5) | P(10) | * | * |
| Pop flies | | | T(5) | * | P(10) | * | * | * |
| Grounders | | | T(5) | * | * | * | * | * |
| Drills | P(15) | P(15) | | P(10) | | P(15) | P(10) | P(10) |
| **Pitching** | | | T(10) | | P(15) | P(10) | P(15) | * |
| Drills | | | P(10) | | | | | P(10) |
| **Hitting** | | | | | | | | |
| Swinging | | | T(10) | P(5) | * | * | P(15) | * |
| Bunting | | | | | | T(10) | * | |
| Sacrificing | | | | | | | | T(5) |
| Drills | | | P(20) | | P(15) | P(10) | | P(15) |
| **Baserunning** | | | | | | | | |
| Rounding bases | | | T(5) | * | * | * | * | * |
| Leadoffs | | | | | | | | |
| Sliding | | | | | | | | |
| Stealing | | | | | | | | |
| Drills | | | | | | | | |
| **Team defense** | | | | | | | | |
| Infield | | | | T(10) | | P(10) | | P(10) |
| Outfield | | | | | | | T(10) | P(10) |
| Drills | | | | P(15) | | P(20) | | |

| Skills | Week 5 | | Week 6 | | Week 7 | | Week 8 | |
|---|---|---|---|---|---|---|---|---|
| | Day 1 | Day 2 | Day 1 | Day 2 | Day 1 | Day 2 | Day 1 | Day 2 |
| Warm-up | (10) | (10) | (10) | (10) | (10) | (10) | (10) | (10) |
| Cool-down | (5) | (5) | (5) | (5) | (5) | (5) | (5) | (5) |
| Evaluation | (5) | (5) | (5) | (5) | (5) | (5) | (5) | (5) |
| **Rules** | * | * | * | * | * | * | * | * |
| Signals | | | T(10) | T(10) | P(10) | * | * | * |
| **Throwing** | * | * | * | * | * | * | * | * |
| Drills | | P(10) | | | | | | |
| **Catching** | | | | | | | | |
| Throws | * | * | * | * | * | * | * | * |
| Pitches | * | * | * | * | * | * | * | * |
| Pop flies | * | * | * | * | * | * | * | * |
| Grounders | * | * | * | * | * | * | * | * |
| Drills | | | P(10) | | | | | |
| **Pitching** | * | * | * | * | * | * | * | * |
| Drills | | | | | | P(10) | | P(10) |
| **Hitting** | | | | | | | | |
| Swinging | P(15) | | * | P(10) | P(20) | P(10) | P(20) | P(15) |
| Bunting | P(15) | P(10) | * | * | * | P(10) | * | * |
| Sacrificing | * | * | * | * | * | | * | * |
| Drills | | | | | | P(10) | P(10) | P(10) |
| **Baserunning** | | | | | | | | |
| Rounding bases | * | * | * | * | * | * | * | * |
| Leadoffs | | T(5) | P(5) | * | * | * | * | * |
| Sliding | | T(10) | P(5) | * | * | * | * | * |
| Stealing | | | T(10) | P(10) | P(10) | * | * | * |
| Drills | | P(10) | P(10) | | | P(10) | P(10) | |
| **Team defense** | | | | | | | | |
| Infield | P(15) | * | P(10) | P(10) | * | * | P(10) | * |
| Outfield | * | P(15) | * | P(10) | * | * | P(10) | * |
| Drills | | | P(20) | P(20) | P(15) | P(20) | | P(15) |

*Note.* Because many skills are practiced simultaneously, a total time for practices is not given. However, we recommend that youth baseball practices last no longer than 90 minutes.

# Baseball and Coaching Books

## Coaching Young Athletes

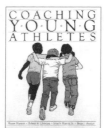

Rainer Martens, PhD,
Robert W. Christina, PhD,
John S. Harvey, Jr., MD, and
Brian J. Sharkey, PhD

1981 ■ Paper ■ 224 pp
Item BMAR0024
ISBN 0-931250-24-2
$18.00 ($22.50 Canadian)

*Coaching Young Athletes* introduces and explains the basics of coaching, such as coaching philosophy, sport psychology, sport pedagogy, sport physiology, sports medicine, parent management, and sport law. You'll find exercises, examples, discussion topics, illustrations, and checklists designed to make learning how to be a more effective coach interesting and enjoyable.

## Hit and Run Baseball

Rod Delmonico, MEd

*Foreword by Ron Fraser, Head Coach, University of Miami*

1992 ■ Paper ■ 184 pp
Item PDEL0327
ISBN 0-88011-327-8
$15.95 ($19.95 Canadian)

This insightful guide on baseball offense will help any team manufacture runs without the benefit of big hits. Rod Delmonico shows coaches how to make things happen while at bat or on base. He details the drills and skills, as well as the advanced insights, you need to develop an aggressive baseball offense.

## Coaching Pitchers

(Second Edition)

Joe "Spanky" McFarland, MS

1990 ■ Paper ■ 152 pp
Item PMCF0368
ISBN 0-88011-368-5
$20.95 ($25.95 Canadian)

*Coaching Pitchers* is a complete coach's guide to pitching for youth, junior high, high school, and college baseball. Coaches will especially appreciate the in-depth information on which exercises and combinations of pitches are best suited to bring a pitcher to the fullest potential possible for a given age and stage of development.

## Coaching Baseball

*Skills and Drills*

Bragg A. Stockton, EdD

1984 ■ Paper ■ 168 pp
Item BSTO0065
ISBN 0-931250-65-X
$18.00 ($22.50 Canadian)

Tackle the complexities of coaching advanced baseball with this invaluable coaches guide. Bragg Stockton, former head coach at the University of Houston, covers all the basics on batting and fielding, scouting and conditioning, coaching and teaching fundamentals, game-winning offensive and defensive strategies, and methods of motivation, encouragement, and reinforcement.

## ACEP Volunteer Level

The American Coaching Effectiveness Program (ACEP) now provides two excellent youth coaches' courses: the Rookie Coaches Course and the Coaching Young Athletes Course. The Rookie Coaches Course not only introduces coaches to the basic principles of coaching, but also teaches them how to apply those fundamentals as they instruct young athletes in the rules, skills, and strategies of their particular sport. This *Rookie Coaches Baseball Guide* serves as a text for the course.

The second coaching education option at the Volunteer Level is the Coaching Young Athletes Course. This alternative is for coaches who have completed the Rookie Coaches Course successfully and coaches who want to receive more instruction in the principles of coaching than is offered in that course.

ACEP encourages youth sport coaches to complete both the Rookie Coaches and Coaching Young Athletes courses. We believe the combined learning experiences afforded by these courses will give you the coaching background you need to be the kind of coach kids learn from and enjoy playing for. Call the ACEP National Center at 1-800-747-4457 for more information on the Volunteer Level.

*Prices subject to change.*

Place your credit card order today! (VISA, AMEX, MC)
TOLL FREE: U.S. (800) 747-4457 ■ Canada (800) 465-7301
OR: U.S. (217) 351-5076 ■ Canada (519) 944-7774
FAX: U.S. (217) 351-1549 ■ Canada (519) 944-7614

**Human Kinetics Publishers**
Box 5076 • Champaign, IL 61825-5076